RALPH STORER is an experienced and respected hillwalker who has hiked and backpacked extensively around the world. Despite being a Sassenach, he has lived in Scotland for many years and has a great affinity for the Highlands, where he can be seen in all weathers roaming the glens and tramping the tops. He wishes to make it clear, however, that hillwalking is only one of many passions in his life.

By the same author

100 Best Routes on Scottish Mountains (Warner Books)
50 Best Routes on Skye and Raasay (Warner Books)
Exploring Scottish Hill Tracks (Warner Books)
The Joy of Hillwalking (Luath Press)
Mountain Trivia Challenge (Cordee)
The World's Great Adventure Treks (contributor) (New Holland)
The Rumpy Pumpy Quiz Book (Metro Publishing)
Love Scenes (a novel) (Mercat Press)

50 Classic Routes
on Scottish Mountains

Revised and Updated

RALPH STORER

Luath Press Limited

EDINBURGH

www.luath.co.uk

First published in hardback by David & Charles 1998
Revised paperback edition 2005

The paper used in this book is recyclable. It is made from low
chlorine pulps produced in a low energy, low emission manner
from renewable forests.

Printed and bound by
Nørhaven Paperback A/S, Viborg, Denmark

Typeset by S. Fairgrieve

To those who follow in our footsteps

A message from the Publishers

Acknowledgements

INVESTIGATING A ROUTE for a hillwalking guidebook involves more than simply climbing a mountain. It may mean exploring more than one approach, checking different ascent routes, pausing repeatedly to take notes, redescending to find a missed path, starting early or chasing a patch of blue sky to obtain the best light for a photograph. It is not the kind of day on the hill that most hillwalkers would be prepared to endure (at least, more than once). I would therefore like all my hillwalking companions to know that, although it may not have seemed like it on occasion, I shall be forever grateful for their patience, understanding and help in the writing of this book.

All maps by Don Sargeant and the author.

All photographs by the author.

Contents

Preface   13
Preface to the Revised Paperback Edition   15

Introduction   17

    Routes   18
    Map Symbols   19
    Sketch Maps   20
    Measurements   21
    Mountain Names   21
    Assessment and Seasonal Notes   22
    Route Difficulty   23
    Access   24

THE SOUTHERN HIGHLANDS   27

1   Ben Vorlich (Arrochar)   28
2   Ben Vane   30
3   Beinn Ime and Beinn Narnain   32
4   Beinn an Lochain   34
5   Ben Oss and Beinn Dubhchraig   36
6   Ben Challum   38
7   Beinn Achaladair and Beinn a' Chreachain   40
8   Creag Mhor   42
9   Stuchd an Lochain   44
10 The Glen Lyon Horseshoe   46

THE CENTRAL HIGHLANDS   49

11 Beinn a' Chochuill and Beinn Eunaich   50
12 Stob Coir' an Albannaich and Glas Bheinn Mhor   52
13 Beinn Sgulaird   54

14	Beinn Fhionnlaidh	56
15	Sgor na h-Ulaidh	58
16	Creise and Meall a' Bhuiridh	60
17	The Giant's Staircase of Stob Ban	62
18	The Treig Traverse	64
19	Carn Dearg and Sgor Gaibhre	66
20	The Ardverikie Trio	68
21	Beinn a' Chaorainn	70

THE WESTERN HIGHLANDS 73

22	Beinn Resipol	74
23	Sgurr Dhomhnuill	76
24	Sgurr Ghiubhsachain	78
25	Gulvain	80
26	Sgurr na h-Aide	82
27	Sgurr nan Coireachan	84
28	Sgurr Mor	86
29	Meall na Teanga	88
30	The Druim Chosaidh	90
31	Ben Aden	92
32	Gairich	94
33	Sgurr a' Mhaoraich	96
34	The South Glen Shiel Ridge	98
35	The Conbhairean Group	100

THE NORTHERN HIGHLANDS 103

36	The Round of the Hundred Hills	104
37	Beinn Dearg (Torridon)	106
38	Beinn an Eoin	108
39	The West Fannichs	110
40	The Glensguaib Circuit	112
41	Cul Mor	114
42	Arkle	116

THE CAIRNGORMS 119

43	Glas Tulaichean	120
44	Broad Cairn	122
45	The Glen Feshie Hills	124
46	The Devil's Point	126
47	Beinn Mheadhoin	128
48	Beinn a' Bhuird	130

THE ISLANDS 133

49	Ullaval and Oreval (Harris)	134
50	Teilesval and Uisgnaval Mor (Harris)	136

Glossary / Index 139

Preface

FOLLOWING ON FROM *50 Best Routes on Scottish Mountains*, *50 More Routes on Scottish Mountains* and *50 Best Routes on Skye and Raasay*, *50 Classic Routes on Scottish Mountains* completes a selection of 200 routes that represents the best of Scottish hill-walking.

50 Classic Routes describes some outstanding walking and scrambling routes that were prevented by lack of space from inclusion in earlier volumes in the series. These routes again range across the Highlands to provide a cross-section of route types and locations, with tedious and tiresome Munro bagging ascent routes avoided in favour of more rewarding ways up. Herein you will find descriptions of popular routes up popular mountains alongside descriptions of interesting ways up less well-known mountains that will be a revelation even to many experienced Scottish hillwalkers.

The temptation to revisit favourite mountains from earlier volumes in order to describe other ascent routes has been resisted. All routes in this volume are brand new, with a greater concentration than before on the easily accessible southern half of the country. Further route possibilities remain, of course, but given the number of mountains in Scotland, a worthwhile continuation of the series would require a change to the route criteria noted in the Introduction. For instance, there are many fine routes on hills that do not meet the 2,000ft/600m height criterion, especially in the Islands.

May the routes presented herein continue to bring you as much joy as they have the author.

Preface to the Revised Paperback Edition

THE FOUR VOLUMES of fifty routes were originally published as four hardbacks by David and Charles. In paperback form, *50 Best Routes* and *50 More Routes* have been combined into *100 Best Routes on Scottish Mountains* and, together with *50 Best Routes on Skye and Raasay*, published by Warner Books.

This Luath Press edition of *50 Classic Routes on Scottish Mountains*, which completes the paperback series, follows seven years on from the hardback edition and incorporates a number of changes. If you think mountain routes wouldn't change much in such a period of time, think again. Lower down, there are new paths, new Land Rover tracks, new starting points, new access arrangements (owing, for example, to afforestation or changes in land ownership)... Higher up, paths can become worn and dangerous, or upgraded and made easier by path maintenance schemes.

Here are some examples of the kind of changes that have occurred in the past seven years. Inverpolly National Nature Reserve now no longer exists (Route 41), the Land Rover track from Dalmunzie Hotel to Glenlochsie Farm has been paved (Route 43), a bulldozed Land Rover track has obliterated the fine old path up Glen Ure (Route 13) and the path up Beinn Dubhchraig is now so eroded that it could do with being obliterated (Route 5).

If route information has changed, the original description has been kept, for the most part, and the route annotated with Update Notes. This solution serves the dual purpose of maintaining parity with the original hardback description and highlighting what changes have taken place.

In addition, there are a number of minor textual differences from the hardback edition. Amendments have been made to correct typographical errors and accommodate a different page design.

For routes 25, 28, 39, 48 and 50, grids have been updated and amended to correct transcription errors. References to the hardback editions *50 Best Routes* and *50 More Routes* have been changed to references to the paperback edition *100 Best Routes*.

A major recent development has been a reappraisal of access to Scotland's countryside, not only in terms of statutory rights but also in terms of the willingness of landowners to countenance the presence of hillwalkers on the land – see Access notes in the Introduction.

Finally, it's worth noting that, in the past few years, more and more car parks at the start of routes have become pay-and-display, e.g. Glen Muick (Route 44) and Linn of Dee (Route 46), so keep a few £1 coins handy.

Introduction

THE MOUNTAIN WALKER in Scotland is spoilt for choice. In the Highlands there are 284 Munros (separate mountains over 3,000ft/914m), a further 227 Tops over 3,000ft/914m, 221 Corbetts (separate mountains over 2,500ft/762m) and countless lesser heights – enough to last a lifetime and more.

The volumes in the *Best Routes* series contain a personal choice of the best walking and scrambling routes in this mountain playground, from short afternoon rambles to day-long expeditions, from roadside summits to remote mountain sanctuaries, from gentle paths to kneebreakingly-steep hillsides, from hands-in-pockets-whistle-while-you-walk strolls to thrilling scrambles.

Any book of this nature begs the question 'What constitutes *best*?', for beauty lies in the eye of the beholder. Some walkers may prefer the vast windswept plateaux of the Cairngorms in winter, others the sharp peaks of Skye on a long summer gloaming. For the purposes of this series, the routes chosen are those I have found to be most enjoyable, would most want to repeat and would most recommend to newcomers, given the following constraints:

1   A route must ascend a mountain over 2,000ft/600m. The fascination with Munros has for too long led to the neglect of some superb smaller mountains; of the 50 routes in this volume, 14 are on mountains under 3,000ft/914m.

2   A route must contain no rock climbing (i.e. on which a rope would normally be required). This does not exclude some scrambles on which walkers of a nervous disposition would never venture – even with a safety net.

3   A route must start from a place that can be reached by motorised transport (plus a ferry if necessary), and end at the same place. There are too many guidebooks whose routes

begin in the middle of nowhere and end somewhere else in the middle of nowhere.

4　A route must be able to be completed by walkers of reasonable fitness in a single day. This does not exclude some routes whose completion may be impracticable in daylight in winter.

5　The overall list of routes must represent a cross-section of all Highland regions. Fifty routes in the Islands, no matter how attractive, would be unsuitable for a guidebook to the best of Scotland.

The list of suggested routes has already provoked many hours of heated debate among colleagues, and may it continue to do so among readers. Yet the amount of agreement is surprising, so much so that I would venture to say that most experienced Scottish walkers would agree with the vast majority of mountains chosen (if not the exact routes). May the following pages while away many an hour in planning, anticipation and reflection.

Routes

The 50 routes are divided into six regions in accordance with accepted geographical divisions and common usage:

The Southern Highlands:	10 routes	–	Routes 1 – 10
The Central Highlands:	11 routes	–	Routes 11 – 21
The Western Highlands:	14 routes	–	Routes 22 – 35
The Northern Highlands:	7 routes	–	Routes 36 – 42
The Cairngorms:	6 routes	–	Routes 43 – 48
The Islands:	2 routes	–	Routes 49 – 50

Within each region routes are listed in approximately south-to-north, west-to-east order.

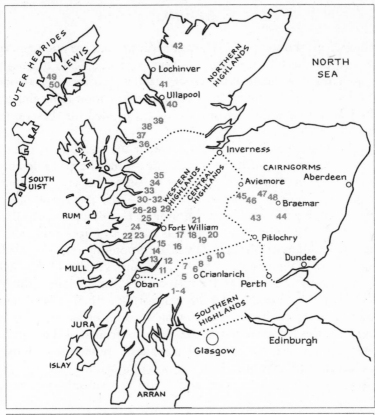

MAP SYMBOLS

▲   Munro

△   Top (in Munro's Tables)

●   Other summit over 3000'/914m

○   Summit over 2500'/762m

▣   Summit over 2000'/610m

□   Summit under 2000'/610m

⊔⊔⊔⊔⊔   Cliff

⌒⌒⌒   River

♦♦♦   Waterfall

~~ ~~ ~~   Route

≡≡≡≡   Landrover track

- - - -   Other paths, tracks, etc.

══════   Road accessible to public

+++++   Railway

++●++   Railway Station

■   Building

  Freshwater Loch

  Sea/Sea Loch

Sketch maps

Sketch maps show each route's major features but are not intended for use on the hill. Ordnance Survey 1:50,000 scale maps are suitable for most Scottish mountain walking, but the os 1:25,000 Outdoor Leisure maps to the Cuillin and Torridon Hills and the High Tops of the Cairngorms are recommended for these more complex areas.

Beside each sketch map is indicated the number of the os 1:50,000 map on which the route appears and the grid reference of the route's starting point (e.g. route 1 – os: 56, GR 319151). Some routes overlap two os maps (e.g. route 25 – os: 40/41) and others appear on either of two maps (e.g. route 21 – os: 34 or 41/42).

The classification of mountains as Munros or Tops is based on the 1997 edition of Munro's Tables, incorporating revisions made since the 1891 publication of Sir Hugh Munro's original list, which contained 283 Munros and a further 255 Tops. Many walkers (including the author) regret any tampering with Sir Hugh's list, apart from reclassification following revision of heights on the map, but the latest edition is the *de facto* arbiter of the Tables. There are no clear criteria of what makes a mountain a Munro, a Top or neither, beyond the definition of a Munro as a separate mountain over 3,000ft/914m and a Top as a subsidiary summit over 3,000ft/914m.

Measurements

Route distances are specified in both miles (to the nearest half-mile) and kilometres (to the nearest kilometre); short distances in the text are specified in metres (an approximate imperial measurement is yards).

Mountain heights are specified in metres and feet. Metric heights have been obtained from os 2nd Series 1:50,000 maps. These may differ slightly from the latest heights obtained by GPS survey. Equivalent heights in feet have been obtained by multiplying the height in metres by 3.28 (rounded down); these may not tally with heights on old os one-inch-to-the-mile maps, which were obtained from an earlier survey.

The total amount of ascent for the whole route is specified to the nearest 10m (50ft). This is an approximation based on os map heights and contours, which are shown at 10m intervals and are in many instances omitted because of cartographic complexity.

Route times (to the nearest half-hour) are based on the time it should take a person of reasonable fitness to complete the route in good summer conditions. They take into account length of route, amount of ascent, technical difficulty, type of terrain and short stoppages, but do not make allowances for long stoppages and adverse weather. They are roughly standard between routes for comparison purposes and can be adjusted where necessary by a factor appropriate to the individual.

In winter, routes will normally take much longer, depending on snow and ice conditions. A pre-dawn start is often necessary and some of the longer routes are best tackled as two-day expeditions, camping en route or making use of a bothy.

Mountain names

Most Highland names are Gaelic in origin and the ability to pronounce and understand Gaelic names can add much to the pleasure of walking in Scotland. To this end a guide to the pronunciation and meaning of all mountain names, and (where space allows) to many other physical features named in the text, is provided in a Glossary/Index.

The production of such a guide is made difficult by a number of factors. os maps, despite their otherwise excellence, appear to have been named by Sassenachs, for they abound in Gaelic misspellings, misunderstandings, misuses and misplacements. With some misgivings the os spelling has been retained for the purpose of standardisation.

Some OS misspellings make pronunciation impossible. Coire Sgreumh (route 35), for instance, is possibly a misspelling of Coire Sgreamh (meaning 'disgust', and perhaps referring to the corrie's agricultural worthlessness); any attempt at a direct pronunciation would be ludicrous. In addition some names have become anglicised to such an extent that it would be pedantic to enforce a purist pronunciation on a non-Gaelic speaker; e.g. the correct pronunciation of Ben is something akin to Pane, with a soft *n* as in the first syllable of *onion*. Moreover, pronunciation differs, sometimes markedly, throughout the Highlands and Islands.

Despite these problems the phonetic guide given in the Glossary should enable a good attempt at a pronunciation that would be intelligible to a Gaelic speaker. In connection with the guide, the following points should be noted:

Y   before a vowel pronounced as in *you*
OW   pronounced as in *town*
CH   pronounced as in Scottish *loch* or German *noch*
TCH   pronounced as *ch* in *church*
OE   pronounced as in French *oeuf* or the *u* in *turn*

Toponymy (the study of place name meanings) is complicated by OS misspellings, changes in spelling and word usage over the centuries, words with more than one meaning, and unknown origin of names (Gaelic, Norse, Irish etc). For example, consider the origin of the name 'Sgurr Cos na Breachd-laoidh' (route 27). Meanings given in this book are the most commonly accepted, even if disputed; when the meaning is doubtful it is annotated with 'poss' (i.e. possible); some names are too obscure to be given any meaning.

Assessment and Seasonal Notes

The assessment is intended as a brief overview of the nature of the route during summer conditions. Under snow, Scottish mountains become much more serious propositions. Paths are obliterated, grassy hillsides become treacherous slopes, ridges become corniced, stone shoots become snow gullies, walking becomes more difficult and tiring, terrain becomes featureless in adverse weather, and white-outs and spindrift reduce visibility to zero.

Winter conditions vary from British to Alpine to Arctic from November through to April, though sometimes earlier and later and varying from locality to locality – it is possible to encounter hard snow and ice even in October and May. No one should venture into the Scottish mountains in winter without adequate clothing, an ice axe and experience (or the company of an experienced person). In hard winter conditions crampons will also be required. The number of accidents – many of them fatal – that occur in Scotland each winter should leave no one in doubt as to the need for caution.

Many of the routes in this book become major mountaineering expeditions in winter and should not be attempted by walkers; such routes are indicated in Seasonal Notes. The viability of other routes in winter depends on grade and conditions; in general the higher the summer grade the higher the winter grade. Note, however, that even a normally straightforward winter route may be subject to avalanche or hard ice, to say nothing of potentially life-threatening, severe winter weather.

The Scottish mountains in winter have an Alpine attraction and reward the prepared walker with unforgettable experiences but, if in doubt, stay off the hill. Bearing these points in mind, the Seasonal Notes for each route indicate any specific places where particular difficulties are normally likely to be encountered, thus enabling the walker to be better prepared. Where an easier escape route presents itself this also is noted.

Route difficulty

The overall difficulty of each route is shown in the form of a grid, as explained on page 25. It will be apparent from this grading system that not all the routes in this book are for novices. Many accidents in the Scottish hills are caused by walkers attempting routes outside their capabilities, and the grading system is intended to enable a more realistic route appraisal. On the more technically difficult routes, easier alternatives are noted in the text or in the Seasonal Notes, if applicable.

Access

Land access has been revolutionised by The Land Reform (Scotland) Act 2003 and the accompanying Scottish Outdoor Access Code (2005), which create a statutory right of responsible access for outdoor recreation. It is recommended that anyone walking in the Scottish countryside familiarise himself/herself with the code, which explains rights and responsibilities in detail. In summary, everyone has a statutory right of access, but:

- Take responsibility for your actions.
- Respect people's privacy and peace of mind.
- Help land managers and others to work safely and effectively.
- Care for your environment.
- Keep your dog under proper control.
- Take extra care if you are organising an event or running a business, and ask the landowner's advice.

More information is available on the website http://www.outdooraccess-scotland.com. Alternatively, contact Scottish Natural Heritage (SNH), which manages the site, at 12 Hope Terrace, Edinburgh EH9 2AS (tel: 0131-447-4784).

Notwithstanding the new access legislation, a further note on deer stalking is warranted. Whatever one's ethical stance on stalking, the fact remains that most of the land in the Scottish Highlands is privately owned, and non-compliance with stalking restrictions is likely to be counter-productive and lead to the imposition of further restrictions. In addition, if estate revenue is lost because of interference with stalking activities, the alternative may be afforestation or worse – which would not only increase access problems but could irreparably alter the landscape.

The red stag stalking season runs from 1 July to 20 October, but actual dates vary from locality to locality. Access notices dot the roadside and information on stalking activities can be obtained from estate offices and head stalkers. For a complete list of dates and estate addresses see *Heading For The Hills*, a booklet published by The Mountaineering Council of Scotland.

To improve communication between stalkers and hillwalkers, an increasing number of estates contribute to the Hillphones service, which provides daily recorded messages of where stalking is taking place. Information on this service can be found on the above outdooraccess-scotland website or on the Hillphones website www.hillphones.info. Alternatively, leaflets can be obtained from The Mountaineering Council of Scotland, The Old Granary, Perth PH1 5QP. It is also worth noting that there is no stalking on a Sunday.

Land belonging to public bodies such as the National Trust for Scotland and the John Muir Trust is normally not subject to stalking restrictions. OS maps show NTS boundaries but may not be up to date.

Finally it should be noted that all river directions given in the text as 'left bank' and 'right bank', in accordance with common usage, refer to the direction when facing downstream.

Grid

	1	2	3	4	5
GRADE	X				
TERRAIN		X			
NAVIGATION			X		
SERIOUSNESS	X				

An at-a-glance grid for each route indicates the route's overall difficulty, where difficulty consists not only of **grade** (i.e., technical difficulty) but also type of **terrain** (irrespective of grade), difficulty of **navigation** with a compass in adverse weather and **seriousness** (i.e. difficulty of escape in case of curtailment of route for one reason or another, based on criteria of length and restricted line of escape). These factors vary over the duration of the route and should not be taken as absolute, but they provide a useful general guide and enable comparisons to be made between routes. Each category is graded 1 (easiest) to 5 (hardest).

Grade
1 Mostly not too steep
2 Appreciable steep sections
3 Some handwork required
4 Easy scramble
5 Hard scramble

Terrain
1 Excellent, often on paths
2 Good
3 Reasonable
4 Rough
5 Tough

Navigation
1 Straightforward
2 Reasonably straightforward
3 Appreciable accuracy required
4 Hard
5 Extremely hard

Seriousness
1 Straightforward escape
2 Reasonably straightforward escape
3 Appreciable seriousness
4 Serious
5 Very serious

The
Southern Highlands

ROUTE 1   **BEN VORLICH (ARROCHAR)**

	1	2	3	4	5
GRADE	X				
TERRAIN		X			
NAVIGATION		X			
SERIOUSNESS	X				

OS MAP: 56
GR: 319151
DISTANCE: 10km (6 miles)
ASCENT: 1,070m (3,500ft)
TIME: 6 hours
ASSESSMENT: A skyline circuit of a beautiful corrie, combining rugged scenery with picturesque views.
SEASONAL NOTES: In winter an ascent via Coire Creagach normally presents no especial difficulties for those competent on snow. An ascent via the north-east ridge, as described, should cause little more difficulty, except when the rocks are iced. Steeper snow slopes may be encountered on the Little Hills traverse.
FISSURE NOTE: On the western slopes of Ben Vorlich, high above Loch Sloy dam, are some curious clefts known as the Vorlich Fissures. View them and visit similar features on route 2.

THE ARROCHAR ALPS, a group of rugged peaks that huddle on the north-west shores of Loch Lomond, are among the most popular mountains in the Highlands. The most spectacular mountain in the group is The Cobbler (Route 1 in *100 Best Routes*); this book recommends four further routes.

Ben Vorlich (not to be confused with Loch Earn's Ben Vorlich further east) is the largest, if not the highest, of the group's four Munros. It is formed of crescent-shaped ridges that arc north-eastwards and south-eastwards from the summit to the shores of Loch Lomond. A further ridge runs directly eastwards from the summit, over the two steep cones known as the Little Hills, to divide this side of the mountain into two beautiful corries: Coire Creagach and Coire Baintighearna.

The route described here circuits Coire Creagach. It begins on the A82 Loch Lomond road at the second railway underpass south of Ardlui station (park in the lay-by opposite the station and walk about 300m south along the road). A path goes through the underpass and rises diagonally across the hillside to climb into Coire Creagach high above the richly wooded, deep-cut glen of the stream that drains it. The path can become quite boggy after rain.

Higher up, a small dam is reached on a side stream that comes down from the bealach between Ben Vorlich's north top and Stob nan Coinnich Bhacain. The path continues left into upper Coire Creagach but a more interesting route, with better going and views, follows the side stream up to the bealach.

From here the broad and increasingly rocky north-east ridge climbs to the north top; stay close to the edge for an occasional scramble or stroll up the path further to the right. The main summit lies ten minutes beyond the north top and there is a trig pillar a short distance further along.

To descend, go eastwards down grassy slopes onto craggier ground, where a path finds the easiest route to the foot of the two Little Hills. On the traverse of the first, keep left to avoid crags on the way up and again on the way down, where a direct descent is barred by two tiers of cliffs. Another steep ascent gains the second top, a stunning viewpoint from where the whole of Loch Lomond seems to be directly beneath your feet.

Turning left, the ridge descends towards Ardlui, steeply at first and then more steadily. At the first trees another craggy steepening leads down to an electrified fence (don't panic – there's a protected stile). Below the next (and last) steepening, keep left on the diminishing rim of the steep-sided glen and cross the river when convenient to rejoin the outward path.

ROUTE 2 BEN VANE

	1	2	3	4	5
GRADE			X		
TERRAIN		X			
NAVIGATION			X		
SERIOUSNESS	X				

OS MAP: 56
GR: 318093
DISTANCE: 12km (7½ miles)
ASCENT: 880m (2,900ft)
TIME: 5 hours

ASSESSMENT: An entertainingly direct ascent of a craggy little Arrochar Alp, with scrambling opportunities to suit all tastes.

SEASONAL NOTES: In winter Ben Vane's east-south-east ridge becomes a series of steep, exposed snow slopes that require care. The descent route described, via the Ben Vane – Beinn Dubh Bealach, offers a more straightforward approach.

WARCRY NOTE: 'Loch Sloy' was the warcry of the Clan MacFarlane, whose ruined castle stands on Inveruglas Isle in Loch Lomond.

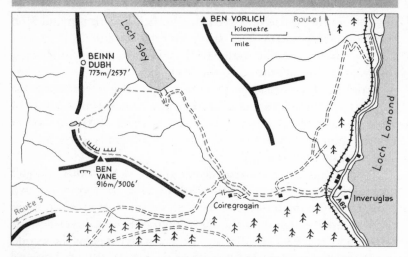

BEN VANE is a steep and craggy little peak with a classically simple shape. Its ascent looks straightforward enough on the map, but the rocky nature of its slopes gives much opportunity for variation. There is a path all the way, although it is steep and fairly exposed in places, and away from it there are numerous opportunities for scrambling. The character and comparative shortness of the ascent make it suitable for a leisurely pace, and this will be encouraged by the many wonderfully positioned natural rock seats that the path passes.

The route begins at Inveruglas on the A82 Loch Lomond road (car park 1km/½ mile north). Follow the paved Loch Sloy hydro-electric access road to the broad basin of Coiregrogain, a wonderfully wild spot with great Highland character at the heart of the Arrochar Alps. When Loch Sloy dam comes into view, turn left to follow a Land Rover track as far as the bridge over the first stream, where the path up Ben Vane's east-south-east ridge begins.

The path climbs left round a crag to reach a flat peaty section, then continues up among minor outcrops to another brief levelling, above which tier upon tier of crags rise to the skyline. Steepening grass leads to the very foot of the lowest crag, then at the last moment the path thankfully veers right and climbs a steep grassy depression to emerge on a cliff edge overlooking Loch Sloy.

From here the path veers back left to regain the ridge before climbing pleasantly among smaller outcrops to a false top, beyond which a couple of steep steps lead to the small round plateau summit. It is necessary to put hand to rock on occasion, but there are no difficulties unless you seek them out; scramblers are left to their own devices.

For a different and less steep return route, descend easy slopes trending north-west then north towards the broad saddle linking Ben Vane to the subsidiary top of Beinn Dubh. From the lochan at the near end of the saddle, descend into the fine ice-scoured basin below, which is so rugged and complex that it may be difficult to see the best way out of it.

Aim for the summit of Ben Vorlich ahead until you arrive at the lip of the basin and can make your way down to the left of the stream that drains it. Before descending, it is worth taking a look on the cliff edge left of the stream at the lip of the basin, where there are some deep fissures. Lower down the hillside, cross the stream and trend right to reach Loch Sloy dam and the access road that will take you all the way back to Inveruglas.

ROUTE 3   BEINN IME and BEINN NARNAIN

	1	2	3	4	5
GRADE				X	
TERRAIN					X
NAVIGATION					X
SERIOUSNESS				X	

OS MAP: 56
GR: 318093
DISTANCE: 18km (11 miles)
ASCENT: 1,440m (4,700ft)
TIME: 8 hours

ASSESSMENT: A varied and exciting obstacle course for experienced hillwalkers only, combining a stimulating scramble up a little-known ridge with the best high-level ridge walk in the Arrochar Alps.

SEASONAL NOTES: The north-east ridge of Beinn Ime and the descent route from A' Chrois are difficult propositions under snow. The easiest winter approach to Beinn Ime and Beinn Narnain is from the Bealach a' Mhaim, reached from either Coiregrogain on its north side, or from Loch Long on its south side.

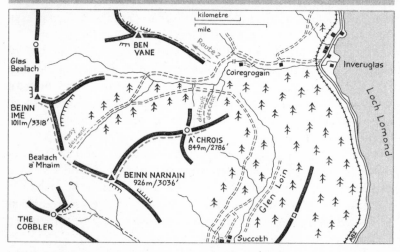

BEINN IME and BEINN NARNAIN are usually climbed by their dull western or southern slopes, but their north-east sides are much more interesting. The north-east ridge of Beinn Ime provides the best ridge scramble in the Arrochar Alps, while the north-east ridge of Beinn Narnain provides the only high-level ridge walk of note in the entire range, ending at the stunning viewpoint of shapely A' Chrois. The route round the two ridges is extremely steep, rugged, devious and adventurous.

Begin at Inveruglas, as for Route 2. Follow the Land Rover

track past Ben Vane and up the narrowing glen of the Allt Coiregrogain, then leave it when it bears left at a small dam and cross the moor to the foot of Beinn Ime's north-east ridge. The crest of the ridge bristles with a succession of large crags, each of which may require trial and error to determine whether a frontal assault or a bypass to left or right is the best way up.

The crux of the ascent is the formidable-looking final rock tower, yet this yields surprisingly to a direct assault, thanks to a short hidden gully that breaches the summit crags. The scrambling is technically easy, but exposure and greasy rock may make it seem harder (it is possible to bypass the tower on the right by descending a few hundred feet). Above the tower an easy stroll over the east top to the summit of Beinn Ime calms the nerves.

From the summit, easy-angled slopes of turf and moss descend to the Bealach a' Mhaim, from where there is an easy escape route back down to Coiregrogain. Steeper slopes then rise to the stony summit plateau of Beinn Narnain, perched above the climbers' crag known as Spearhead Buttress. From here the aesthetic continuation of the route is north-eastwards, where a little path takes a pleasing line round numerous rocky knolls on the complex little ridge leading out to A' Chrois.

Be advised, however, that the descent from A' Chrois requires care on very steep slopes and perseverance and a sense of humour in the dense forest below. If in doubt, descend from the Bealach a' Mhaim, as noted above. Otherwise, descend eastwards from A' Chrois round a large grassy bowl towards a point seen lower down.

When convenient, descend into the bowl and aim for the head of the large gully at the centre of its lower rim. Descend the gully beside a stream on very steep, tussocky grass, then bushwhack down through conifers to a forest road. Go left along the road to the next stream, then bushwhack down beside this, cross the Allt Coiregrogain and climb through less dense tree cover on the far side to rejoin the Land Rover track to Inveruglas.

ROUTE 4 **BEINN an LOCHAIN**

	1	2	3	4	5
GRADE			X		
TERRAIN	X				
NAVIGATION	X				
SERIOUSNESS	X				

OS MAP: 56
GR: 235089
DISTANCE: 5km (3 miles)
ASCENT: 700m (2,300ft)
TIME: 4 hours

ASSESSMENT: A short, scenic and extremely enjoyable ascent of one of the best ridges of its grade in the country.

SEASONAL NOTES: In winter, when the path is obliterated by snow, very steep exposed snow slopes will be encountered and iced rock may also be a problem. The north-east corrie is at its most spectacular in such conditions, but the route is not one for inexperienced winter climbers.

HOWFF NOTE: In the bowl of the north-east corrie, two leaning boulders form a shelter known as Sunset Arch.

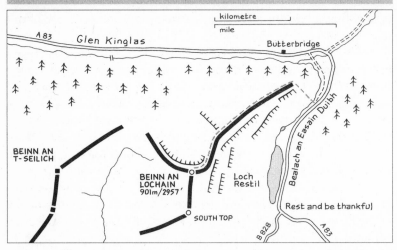

BEINN AN LOCHAIN stands in a commanding position at the junction of three deep glens west of Arrochar. It is separated from the Arrochar Alps by the Bealach an Easain Duibh, where the A83 crosses the Rest and Be Thankful Pass at 246m (807ft) to give a high starting point to the ascent.

The mountain has confused many Munro baggers over the years; the OS originally mapped its height as 2,992ft but Munro remeasured it and included it in his 1891 Tables with a height of 3,021ft, only for it to be demoted by the OS to a 901m (2,957ft)

Corbett in 1981. Whatever its status, it is an attractive little peak whose steep, craggy north and east faces meet at a narrow north-east ridge, which provides a short route to the summit with a real mountaineering flavour and a good path all the way.

To avoid forestry plantations at the very foot of the ridge, begin at the lay-by about 800m north of Loch Restil, the 'lochan' after which the mountain is named. From the small dam on the stream just beyond, a path crosses marshy ground and climbs onto the ridge right of all crags. The ridge rises steadily and is a joy to climb, with occasional minor handwork to add spice to the ascent. It is broad enough to be easy but narrow enough to provide views down each side, westwards to Glen Kinglas and eastwards over crags to Glen Croe.

At 700m (2,300ft) you reach a dip, beyond which a craggy face rears up more steeply. To avoid the crags, the path climbs right across steep, exposed grass slopes and regains the crest of the ridge above the face. A pleasant undulating section then leads to a final steep ascent that is the most exciting part of the route.

The path clings to the very edge of the north-east corrie, whose crags drop away to the right. Look for the odd-looking pinnacle across the corrie. In places the ridge is no wider than the path, and occasional minor handwork is again required, but the path avoids all major obstacles on the left and makes the ascent barely more difficult than what you have done already. The summit cairn arrives all too soon.

Just beyond the summit lies the second of Beinn an Lochain's twin tops. If you wish to extend the route, you can continue from here across a saddle to the south top above Gleann Mor. From here it is possible to make a way down the steep, craggy east face to the roadside south of Loch Restil, but most people will be more than happy to reverse the ascent route, in order to enjoy the north-east ridge for a second time.

ROUTE 5   BEN OSS and BEINN DUBHCHRAIG

	1	2	3	4	5
GRADE	X				
TERRAIN	X				
NAVIGATION				X	
SERIOUSNESS			X		

OS MAP: 50
GR: 344291
DISTANCE: 17km (10½ miles)
ASCENT: 1,170m (3,850ft)
TIME: 7 hours

ASSESSMENT: A gentle ascent leads to a contrastingly rugged traverse across two neighbouring Munros, with superb Southern Highland views.

SEASONAL NOTES: In winter the route is often characterised by a mixture of deep snow in Coire Dubhchraig and windswept, icy terrain on the ridge connecting the two mountains. This ridge is surprisingly complex and requires the negotiation of steep slopes of snow or ice in order to avoid crags.

PATH UPDATE NOTE: Coille Coire Chuilc remains a 'beautiful old pine forest,' but the path up to Coire Dubhchraig is now anything but. As you scuttle around the quagmires, a sense of humour will prove helpful.

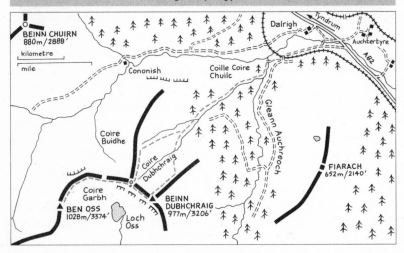

THE STEEP SUMMIT cone of Ben Oss and the craggy south face of Beinn Dubhchraig would normally single out these two neighbouring mountains as prime hillwalking objectives but, in the normal view of them from near Tyndrum to the north, their best features are hidden and the peaks are overshadowed by the classic outlines of nearby Ben Lui (Route 4 in *100 Best Routes*).

Even so, the approach from the northern side has much to recommend it, including a gentle ascent through one of the last remnants of Old Caledonian Pine forest in the Highlands. Once up, the craggy nature of the mountains becomes more apparent, and more rugged terrain awaits on the traverse from one to the other.

The route begins just off the A82 at Dalrigh, 2km (1½ miles) east of Tyndrum. Follow a side road down to a bridge over the River Fillan and continue along a track to another bridge over the West Highland Railway line. On the far side of this bridge, leave the track for a path on the right that crosses boggy ground to a footbridge over the Allt Gleann Auchreoch. Continue beside the stream as far as its confluence with the Allt Coire Dubhchraig, then bear right to follow this stream up into Coire Dubhchraig. If you lose the path, it can be found on the crest of a small ridge right of the stream.

The route climbs through the beautiful old pine forest of Coille Coire Chuilc and up beside newer conifer plantations into the shallow grassy bowl of Coire Dubhchraig, nestled beneath the summit slopes of Beinn Dubhchraig. To make a circuit of the corrie skyline, gain the eastern (left-hand) bounding ridge left of broken crags and climb steeply to the summit on short turf, with wonderful views eastwards to the Crianlarich hills and southwards along the length of Loch Lomond.

The route continues across a bealach to Ben Oss, following a broad ridge above crags fringing Coire Garbh and Loch Oss. A gentle descent to two ridge-top lochans is followed by a very steep descent to the bealach, beset by tiers of small crags that make routefinding difficult in mist. The climb up Ben Oss is in two distinct halves, the ridge rising steeply to a small top before continuing more steadily to the summit.

To return, first retrace your steps to the two lochans at the top of the steep slope on the Beinn Dubhchraig side of the bealach. Head northwards from here to descend the west-bounding ridge of Coire Dubhchraig, then curve down into the corrie to rejoin the outward route.

ROUTE 6 **BEN CHALLUM**

	1	2	3	4	5
GRADE				X	
TERRAIN			X		
NAVIGATION			X		
SERIOUSNESS		X			

OS MAP: 50
GR: 349288
DISTANCE: 14km (8½ miles)
ASCENT: 900m (2,950ft)
TIME: 6 hours
ASSESSMENT: A rocky ridge leads to the summit of a shapely mountain and viewpoint. **Note:** The easiest lines reduce the Grade to 2.

SEASONAL NOTES: The north-west ridge gives a sporting winter ascent. The southern flank of the mountain remains easy, but the ridge connecting the south top to the summit demands respect when corniced. Cornices form on both north and east sides, requiring extreme caution, especially in foul weather.

WET DAY NOTE: Ben Challum is said to be a good hill for a rainy day, as its isolation stops you being tempted onto a second hill.

ACCESS UPDATE NOTE: It's as easy to begin on the Kirkton access track as on the Auchtertyre access track, and there's more roadside parking nearby.

BEN CHALLUM is an attractive but deceptive mountain. From the A82 Crianlarich-Tyndrum road its dreary southern flank provides a seemingly interminable route of ascent for Munro baggers. The true stature of the mountain is revealed only in its northerly aspect, where its conical summit towers over a craggy north face at the head of Glen Lochay. The most interesting route to the summit climbs the rocky north-west ridge on the western edge of this face.

Begin at the short access road to Auchtertyre, at the bridge over the River Fillan 2½ km (1½ miles) east of Tyndrum. From Auchtertyre, follow a Land Rover track up the left-hand side of the tree-lined gorge of the Allt Gleann a' Chlachain. At a junction of glens at the foot of Beinn Chaorach, the track crosses the Allt a' Chaol Ghlinne (bridge) and doubles back to continue up Gleann a' Chlachain well away from the river. Across the glen on the right, the skyline forms the route of descent, with the twin tops of Ben Challum visible at its end.

When the track comes to an abrupt end halfway up the glen, keep going across the grassy hillside. Maintain height until you reach the bowl of the corrie at the head of the glen, then climb easy grass slopes to the Bealach Ghlas Leathaid between Cam Chreag and Ben Challum, where the northern view opens up across Ben Challum's north face to Glen Lochay.

The north-west ridge rises over 440m (1,450ft) from the bealach to the summit. The lower half consists of steep grass and rock outcrops, rising to a conspicuous and problematic-looking rock castle. Bands of crags leading up to the castle give opportunities for excellent scrambling of all grades.

The easiest direct line, staying close beside an old fence at first, is mostly Grade 3 with a few Grade 4 moves, but all scrambling can be avoided on steep grass slopes to the right if you wish. The upper half of the ridge rises more steadily over broken ground to reach the isolated summit, which offers wonderful Southern Highland views all round the compass.

Turning southwards at the summit, the descent route follows the Munro baggers' trade route across a pleasantly narrow saddle to the knobbly south top, which can be a confusing place in mist. Beyond here the featureless southern slopes noted above flare out above Strath Fillan. The key to a fast and knee-friendly descent is to stay well left to find a path beside a fence. The fence and path lead down to and across Creag Loisgte, then all the way down to a footbridge over the railway line above Kirkton Farm and a Land Rover track back to Auchtertyre.

ROUTE 7   BEINN ACHALADAIR and BEINN a' CHREACHAIN

	1	2	3	4	5
GRADE		X			
TERRAIN	X				
NAVIGATION				X	
SERIOUSNESS			X		

OS MAP: 50
GR: 322443
DISTANCE: 18km (11½ miles)
ASCENT: 1,240m (4,050ft)
TIME: 8 hours

ASSESSMENT: Grand ridges, grand corries, grand terrain and grand views add up to a scenic circuit on the southern rim of Rannoch Moor.

SEASONAL NOTES: The ascent of Beinn Achaladair via Coire Achaladair is a good introduction to Scottish winter hillwalking, providing there is no avalanche danger. The route beyond the summit should be left to more experienced winter hillwalkers, owing to the very steep snow slopes that continue down to the next bealach and the narrow snow crest of Beinn a' Chreachain's north-east ridge.

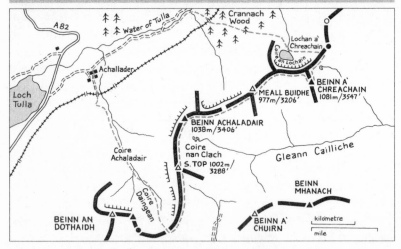

OF THE FIVE Munros that cluster beside Bridge of Orchy, Beinn Dorain and Beinn an Dothaidh have the most appealing roadside frontage (see Route 9 in *100 Best Routes*). Beinn Achaladair and Beinn a' Chreachain are more secretive mountains, their wall-like roadside faces hiding their best features and deterring the unknowledgeable. The pair make a superb round, however, with wonderful ridges to wander along, a magnificent hidden corrie to explore and a return through one of the finest remaining Old Caledonian pinewoods.

Park at Achallader Farm, reached by a track from the shores of Loch Tulla on the A82. From here, follow a track through the farmyard and up to a bridge over the West Highland Railway line. A path continues up the left bank (right side) of the stream into Coire Achaladair and the higher Coire Daingean, between the craggy west wall of Beinn Achaladair and the impressive north-east corrie of Beinn an Dothaidh.

Coire Achaladair and Coire Daingean are no more than shallow scoops in the glen, and the bealach between the two mountains is easily reached. Slopes of grass and moss continue from here up a pleasantly narrowing ridge to Beinn Achaladair's south top and across a saddle to the summit, perched at the cliff edge of another impressive north-east corrie.

Beyond the summit, steep broken slopes descend round the corrie rim to the next bealach, where grassy terrain returns for the ascent of Meall Buidhe, which bars the way to Beinn a' Chreachain. Meall Buidhe's ½-mile long, level summit ridge leads pleasantly onwards above the vast expanse of Rannoch Moor to the rim of the route's finest feature – Coire an Lochain, where craggy buttresses drop 250m (800ft) to the shores of the lochan below. After a short descent, a steady pull up broken slopes above the corrie gains the summit of Beinn a' Chreachain, set a few hundred metres back from the corrie rim.

The summit is the last top of the day, but the most entertaining part of the route is still to come. From the summit, regain the corrie rim and continue round it down a gentle but narrow ridge, with considerable drops on each side. There is no difficulty, but the exposure will not be to everyone's taste. After the ridge broadens onto a saddle, you can descend anywhere into the corrie to reach the lochan.

The return route descends the grassy hillside below the corrie, taking a diagonal line down through the beautiful old pines of Crannach Wood to a bridge over the railway line at GR 349455. From here a path descends to the Water of Tulla and joins a track leading back to Achallader Farm.

ROUTE 8 **CREAG MHOR**

	1	2	3	4	5
GRADE	X				
TERRAIN	X				
NAVIGATION			X		
SERIOUSNESS			X		

OS MAP: 50/51
GR: 461370
DISTANCE: 19km (12 miles)
ASCENT: 830m (2,750ft)
TIME: 7 hours

ASSESSMENT: A pleasant skyline ridge walk, with extensive views, round a deep corrie.

SEASONAL NOTES: A fine narrow winter ridge walk for those competent on snow, normally without any technical difficulties, but beware steep snow slopes that may inhibit ascent to Sron nan Eun and descent from Sail Dhubh at each end of the ridge.

POETIC NOTE: Coire-cheathaich gave inspiration to the renowned Gaelic poet Duncan Ban MacIntyre when he was gamekeeper here in the eighteenth century.

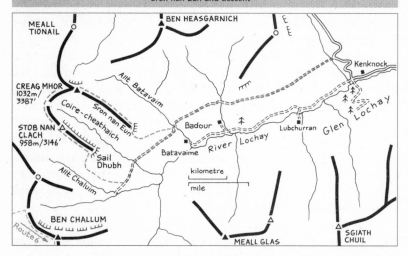

TO THE WEST of Loch Tay, peaceful Glen Lochay threads its serene way westwards to the Forest of Mamlorn, a treeless former royal deer forest that is now no more than a curious name on the map. Dispersed around the glen are six well-separated Munros whose dreary hillsides are among the least appealing in the Southern Highlands. Ben Challum (see Route 6) and Creag Mhor are honourable exceptions.

Even Creag Mhor's Gaelic name (meaning Big Crag), although something of an exaggeration, holds out a promise of more interesting things. To the south-east the mountain throws out two well-defined ridges that enclose and end at abrupt drops above the head of Glen Lochay. The round of the corrie skyline is an excellent ridge walk.

The route begins on the minor road up Glen Lochay. At the junction just beyond Kenknock, the paved road turns right to zigzag up the hillside. Begin 1km (¾ mile) up, where a Land Rover track branches left. Follow the mostly level track across the hillside for 5km (3 miles) to the bridge over the Allt Batavaim, then leave it to climb the ridge leading up to Sron nan Eun. The band of crags low down is most easily turned on the left, to find less steep ground that rises to the crest of the ridge.

At the top of Sron nan Eun the ridge levels off and undulates pleasantly before narrowing and rising again in a series of steps to reach the summit of Creag Mhor. The shapely summit is the apex of three ridges, and thanks to the deep glens all around there are extensive views in all directions. The actual summit is one of a series of stony knolls that can be confusing in mist.

Continuing round the skyline of Coire-cheathaich, broad gentle slopes (which can also be confusing in mist) lead down to a saddle, and then the ridge narrows once more for the short climb up to triple-topped Stob nan Clach, whose first top is its highest. Beyond Stob nan Clach a level section of ridge continues pleasantly above steep drops into the corrie, then a sharp descent leads to another level section and a walk out to Sail Dhubh, the outcrop of rock that marks the end of the round.

Pause for a final breath of mountain air before the steep descent back to the track and the long walk back. A direct descent east-south-east to the foot of the corrie is beset by crags and complicated by the fact that it is on the join of two maps. It is better to descend south-south-west, towards the summit of Ben Challum across the glen, and then contour round the foot of Sail Dhubh to regain the track.

ROUTE 9 **STUCHD an LOCHAIN**

	1 2 3 4 5
GRADE	X
TERRAIN	X
NAVIGATION	X
SERIOUSNESS	X

OS MAP: 51
GR: 500463
DISTANCE: 9km (5½ miles)
ASCENT: 650m (2,150ft)
TIME: 4 hours

ASSESSMENT: A high starting point gives easy access to a seemingly unprepossessing mountain, but one that conceals a great lochan-filled corrie on its hidden northern side and commands panoramic views in a remote setting.

SEASONAL NOTES: In winter, steep snow slopes will be encountered on the ascent route described (and note that it may also be necessary to descend this way). The north ridge offers an exciting winter descent but is not for the inexperienced. The only easy winter route is via the Allt Cashlie.

PATH UPDATE NOTE: On the steep hillside above Loch an Daimh, the worn ascent path becomes very wet after rain and is perhaps best avoided.

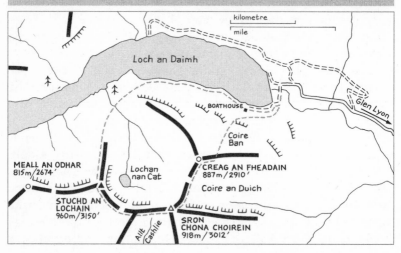

STUCHD AN LOCHAIN has the distinction of hosting the first recorded ascent of a Munro, when it was climbed by 'Mad' Colin Campbell of Glen Lyon about 1590 and its summit described as 'a huge rock beetling over a deep circular mountain tarn'. Some would think you have to be mad to climb mountains, but Stuchd an Lochain has other merits besides its historical pre-eminence.

Although it lacks character when approached by the tedious Munro baggers' route along the Allt Cashlie from the south, its remoteness and isolation from other mountains give it wide-ranging summit views, while on its northern flank it harbours a great corrie where broken rock terraces plunge 250m (800ft) to the circular Lochan nan Cat. A further attraction to some is the ease of the ascent, for few Highland peaks can be approached from a starting height of 400m (1,300ft).

Begin at the foot of Giorra Dam at the eastern end of Loch an Daimh in upper Glen Lyon. Walk up the road to the southern end of the dam and continue along a shoreline track as far as the first right-hand bend. Leave the track here for a path that climbs diagonally across the hillside then steeply up a shallow depression between broken crags, with good views back down the great green broad-bottomed trench of Glen Lyon. The whole hillside above the shoreline is dotted with small crags, so take note of the ascent route in case you decide to return this way.

You reach the skyline on the east ridge of Creag an Fheadain, and from here a broken fence leads all the way to the summit of Stuchd an Lochain. The ridge rises in a couple of steepenings to the summit of Creag an Fheadain, beyond which the northern corrie and its lochan are seen for the first time.

The route bears left round the corrie rim and crosses a saddle to the summit of Sron Chona Choirein (in mist note that the summit cairn lies 30m left of the fence's high point). A path bypasses the top for those in a hurry (perish the thought!). Swinging right again, the route undulates gently down to another saddle before tackling Stuchd an Lochain's steeper summit cone. The summit rewards with a glorious view westwards across perhaps the least trodden country in the Southern Highlands.

For a different and interesting return route, descend the steep north ridge. This is initially narrow and pleasant (unless you suffer from vertigo), and is almost Grade 3 at a couple of steepenings, but a path runs along the crest and there is little difficulty. Lower down, bear right to reach the lochside and follow the shoreline back to the track and dam.

ROUTE 10 **THE GLEN LYON HORSESHOE**

	1	2	3	4	5
GRADE	X				
TERRAIN	X				
NAVIGATION					X
SERIOUSNESS	X				

OS MAP: 51
GR: 666483
DISTANCE: 17km (11 miles)
ASCENT: 1,340m (4,400ft)
TIME: 7½ hours

ASSESSMENT: Four easy Munros + miles of high grassy ridges = a superior stravaig across the sweeping greensward.
SEASONAL NOTES: The complete horseshoe is a major undertaking on a short winter's day, but the benign nature of the mountains makes the ascent of any of them an ideal introduction to Scottish winter hillwalking (in good weather!).
SCENIC NOTE: Glen Lyon lays claim to being the longest and one of the most beautiful glens in Scotland.
NOMENCLATURE UPDATE NOTE: Meall nan Aighean's name continues to cause confusion. The Munro used to be called Creag Mhor, but that name (meaning Big Crag) referred to a different mountain feature and has been replaced in up-to-date guidebooks and maps.

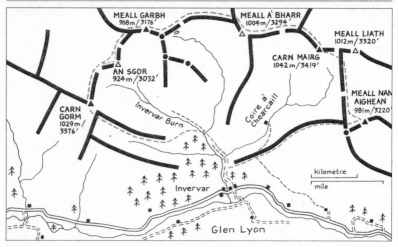

THE FOUR MUNROS that form the Glen Lyon Horseshoe are linked by a 8km (5 mile) long, plateau-like ridge that forms a broad crescent round the small village of Invervar. The ridge sweeps across the skyline from top to top in almost Cairngorm-like fashion, except that the terrain is almost completely grassy. This makes for undistinguished summits but wonderfully easy high-level rambling, in a landscape whose mood is more dependent than most on the weather. The complete round may be either a glorious stravaig or, in foul weather, a routefinding nightmare (although descent to the glen can always be made easily at any point).

The route begins opposite the telephone box in Invervar in Glen Lyon, 8km (5 miles) west of Fortingall. Follow the old cart track on the east bank of the Invervar Burn past a restored lint mill (worth a look) and through a small wood. Once out of the wood, leave the track at the first telegraph pole for an excellent path that climbs Meall nan Aighean's pleasingly angled south-west ridge all the way to the castellated summit (the more westerly of two tops).

Carn Mairg, the group's next and reigning peak, lies north-west across a knolly saddle. The easiest line of ascent appears to be via a higher saddle between Carn Mairg and neighbouring Meall Liath, but the main path veers left before here in order to climb a grassy rake that splits the summit boulderfield. Over the summit, a short descent leads to a stony crest topped by a broken old fence (useful in mist), with the main path keeping below left on the grass. A minor top is passed and then the fence reaches the long flat top of Meall a' Bharr, which gives wonderful walking.

Next comes a descent to a long bealach and a re-ascent to twin-topped Meall Garbh, the third Munro; the western top is the summit. Halfway down to the next bealach the fence veers right and is left behind. An Sgor now bars the way to Carn Gorm, the fourth and final Munro.

In spite of its name, An Sgor is a dull little hill and, as the sight of the ascent of Carn Gorm ahead dissuaded the author from climbing it, you too are allowed to circumvent it on the well-worn bypass path (the ascent adds a further 80m/250ft to the route). The summit cairn of Carn Gorm lies 100m beyond the trig pillar and affords a grand view across the green trench of Glen Lyon to the Lawers group.

The day ends on another good path that descends an occasionally steep ridge to a bridge over the Invervar Burn at the forest edge, and eventually to the cart track back to Invervar.

The
Central Highlands

ROUTE 11   **BEINN a' CHOCHUILL and BEINN EUNAICH**

	1	2	3	4	5
GRADE		X			
TERRAIN		X			
NAVIGATION		X			
SERIOUSNESS		X			

OS MAP: 50
GR: 136288
DISTANCE: 13km (8 miles)
ASCENT: 1,210m (3,950ft)
TIME: 6½ hours

ASSESSMENT: A round of lofty ridges and great views on Ben Cruachan's two unjustly ignored neighbouring Munros.

SEASONAL NOTES: In winter the windswept ridges of both mountains can become icy, and the steep initial ascent and final descent may also prove troublesome under snow. The cornice that forms on Beinn a' Chochuill's summit ridge is sinuous, complex and one of the most beautiful in the Highlands, but it can be very dangerous in a white-out.

INFAMY NOTE: Beinn Eunaich's east face contains the once infamous Black Shoot, a strenuous route first climbed in 1892.

THE TWO MUNROS north of Dalmally would attract more attention were it not for neighbouring Ben Cruachan across the Lairig Noe (Route 13 in *100 Best Routes*). Beinn a' Chochuill especially has a fine, tapering summit ridge that affords superb views of Cruachan's hidden northern corries.

Begin at the bridge over the Allt Mhoille on the B8077 just west of Dalmally and take the Land Rover track on the east (right-hand) side of the river. The track forks left at Castles Farm and rises steadily across the flanks of Beinn Eunaich to provide easy access to Beinn a' Chochuill ahead. After 3km (2 miles) it reaches a junction at the foot of Beinn a' Chochuill's south-east spur – an ill-defined, grassy ridge bounding a shallow corrie.

Leave the track to climb directly up the spur. The ascent is steep, but all will seem worthwhile when you finally breast the east ridge barely 1km (½ mile) from the summit. The view to the north encompasses a whole swathe of Central Highland peaks across remote Glen Kinglass, while to the south Cruachan's magnificent but rarely visited northern corries become ever more impressive, its pointed summit ever more improbable.

The east ridge undulates and curves elegantly as it makes its way westwards to Beinn a' Chochuill's summit, which is reached all too soon. You will want to spend some time here to take in the view, to which is now added a western vista across Loch Etive to the Isle of Mull.

The route to Beinn Eunaich re-descends the whole length of the east ridge to the saddle between the two mountains. The going is delightfully easy on short turf and the path that has developed is hardly necessary. A final steepening deposits you on the saddle and then a stiff 260m (850ft) pull, on steep bouldery slopes near the top, leads to the summit of Beinn Eunaich and yet more superb views, this time eastwards over Glen Strae to the Orchy and Crianlarich mountains.

The descent from the summit is a very pleasant stroll down a broad, easy-angled ridge that leads southwards to the knobbly spur of Stob Maol, with the serene waters of Loch Awe spread before you. To avoid the outcrops that front Stob Maol on its south side, descend right, down steep grass slopes, to rejoin the outward track near Castles Farm.

As you descend, spare a thought for Percy Unna, whose donations to the National Trust enabled the purchase of Glen Coe, Kintail and other areas for future hillwalkers to enjoy. Warned against hillwalking because of a heart condition, the call of the hills proved too much and he died of heart failure while walking alone on Beinn Eunaich in 1950.

ROUTE 12 **STOB COIR' an ALBANNAICH & GLAS BHEINN MHOR**

	1	2	3	4	5
GRADE			X		
TERRAIN				X	
NAVIGATION					X
SERIOUSNESS			X		

OS MAP: 50
GR: 136468
DISTANCE: 17km (10½ miles)
ASCENT: 1,380m (4,550ft)
TIME: 8 hours

ASSESSMENT: An exciting ascent (or an easier Grade 2 alternative) leads to the summit of a massive, sprawling mountain and a tapering ridge walk across its shapely neighbour.

SEASONAL NOTES: Steep snow will be encountered at some point on all winter approaches to the two mountains. The Coire Glas spur becomes a winter mountaineering route that is prone to avalanche. Glas Bheinn Mhor's west ridge makes a fine winter approach, but beware steep snow slopes below the Ben Starav Bealach.

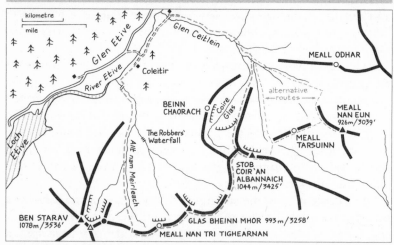

FROM THE ROADSIDE at the foot of Glen Etive, the pyramid-shaped summit of Glas Bheinn Mhor looks an attractive proposition, and its ascent can be combined with a sporting ascent of Stob Coir' an Albannaich, its extremely complex neighbour, to form an interesting round. Begin on the Land Rover track to Coleitir Cottage, 4km (2½ miles) from the road end. One hundred metres beyond the bridge over the River Etive, fork left to reach Glen Ceitlein and then fork right up the almost level glen. The track soon dwindles to a path, which continues up to a great grassy basin hemmed in by mountains.

For a route from here to the summit of Stob Coir' an Albannaich that has a real mountaineering flavour, climb the rough spur that forms the left-hand side of the fine gorge below Coire Glas. A patchwork of granite slabs covers the hillside, with a number of easy-angled rock ribs that give good (optional) friction scrambling. With good routefinding, in dry conditions, the ascent need involve little more than occasional handwork, but in places its steepness may cause discomfort to the nervous.

For an easier-angled ascent, climb up or around slabby ground left of the stream that comes down from the Albannaich-Meall Tarsuinn bealach, then go straight up steep slopes to reach Stob Coir' an Albannaich's east ridge near the summit. For a much longer route that avoids the slabs altogether, continue up to the bealach right of Meall Odhar (the leftmost bump on the skyline ahead), then cross Meall nan Eun (an extremely uninteresting Munro) and Beinn Tarsuinn.

At the top of the Coire Glas spur the ridge tapers pleasantly on excellent terrain and curves round to Stob Coir' an Albannaich's gravelly summit, from where there are wonderful views of the mountains around Glen Etive, Glen Coe and Bridge of Orchy. The route then continues down sprawling grassy slopes to the bealach below Glas Bheinn Mhor, becoming steep and stony near the foot. The ascent of the far side is initially steep and rocky, but a path eases the going.

Soon you find yourself on a tapering ridge that leads pleasantly over the summit of Glas Bheinn Mhor and down the far side to the bealach below Meall nan Tri Tighearnan. A short climb over this last top of the day brings you to the bealach below mighty Ben Starav, which can be added to the route to make a longer day but is more aesthetically approached by its north ridge (see Route 14 in *100 Best Routes*). The day ends with a long descent on an intermittently reasonable path beside the Allt nan Meirleach, which provides good views of the Robbers' Waterfall on its way down to Coleitir.

ROUTE 13 **BEINN SGULAIRD**

	1	2	3	4	5
GRADE			X		
TERRAIN		X			
NAVIGATION			X		
SERIOUSNESS		X			

OS MAP: 50
GR: 010457
DISTANCE: 16km (10 miles)
ASCENT: 1,150m (3,750ft)
TIME: 7½ hours
ASSESSMENT: An intriguing walk across the undulating, twisting, rocky summit ridge of a superbly situated mountain.

SEASONAL NOTES: Beinn Sgulaird is a complex and sporting winter mountain. Entertaining problems for experienced winter walkers include the rocky east ridge, the narrow south ridge (often a beautiful snow arête) and the short sharp ascents of Meall Garbh and Point 863.

HISTORICAL NOTE: The obliterated Glen Ure path was formerly a major line of communication between Glen Etive parish and the west coast.

PATH UPDATE NOTE: (1) When the hardback edition of 50 Classic Routes was researched, the eyesore of a new track up Glen Ure stopped below the wooded gorge. It has now been bulldozed all the way up onto the moors beyond. This is not good. (2) From Point 488, instead of making directly for the roadside, you can now follow a pleasant little path down the south-west ridge. This leads to a Land Rover track that descends beside the Allt Buidhe and through the woods to reach the roadside at GR 459450, beside the north entrance to Druimavuic, just south of the suggested starting point.

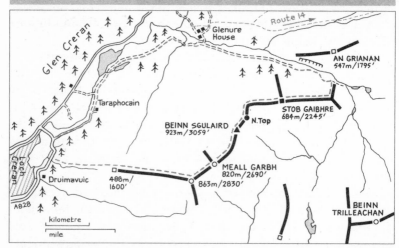

ROUTES 13 TO 15 explore the region west of the Glen Etive/Loch Etive gap, whose rugged hills and mountains are among the least visited in the Central Highlands. The mountains reach Munro status in only three places, yet there is much to interest the hill-walker here, with lots of exposed rock and well-defined ridges that rise invitingly out of remote moorland.

Beinn Sgulaird is the most immediately appealing of the three

Munros. Its many-topped, S-shaped ridge runs for 3km (2 miles) from end to end, providing a glorious stravaig with a spot of scrambling and wonderful west coast views.

Begin on the A828 at the head of Loch Creran. Take the private road up the east side of Glen Creran to Taraphocain and continue along a Land Rover track round the foot of Beinn Sgulaird into Glen Ure. At the fork near Glenure House, keep right on the south side of the river, following an unfortunate new bulldozed track. In the upper glen the river runs through a fine wooded gorge, but the track has obliterated the former historic hill path that wended its way up here onto the moors (see Path Update Note 1).

Eventually you round a corner and obtain a distant view of Stob Coir' an Albannaich (Route 12). Leave the track at its high point, climb the crest of the knoll on the right and continue up grassy slopes, past numerous erratic boulders, to the twin tops of Stob Gaibhre. A short, craggy descent bars the way onward to the foot of the east ridge of Beinn Sgulaird; turn the crags on the right after reversing your steps a short distance. Tackle the ridge directly. It becomes narrower and steeper as it gains height and is characterised by outcrops of broken rock that can be either scrambled up or avoided almost altogether.

At the top you emerge abruptly onto the level summit ridge for a spectacular view across Loch Creran to the Isle of Mull. Stroll along the ridge and scramble over the north top to reach the summit, then continue down the fine, narrow, perfectly angled south ridge, poised above steep drops on each side. Cross a saddle and make a short, steep climb up Meall Garbh, then cross a broader saddle and make another short, steep climb up Point 863 at the end of the main ridge.

The descent goes directly westwards all the way to the roadside, with that glorious view over Loch Creran in front of you the whole way. Go down broad grassy slopes to a dip and the minor irritation of Point 488, then follow the stream that flows down the west side of this top to reach the roadside a few minutes walk from your starting point (but see Path Update Note 2).

ROUTE 14 **BEINN FHIONNLAIDH**

	1	2	3	4	5
GRADE				X	
TERRAIN		X			
NAVIGATION				X	
SERIOUSNESS		X			

OS MAP: 50
GR: 035488
DISTANCE: 16km (10 miles)
ASCENT: 960m (3,150ft)
TIME: 6 hours
ASSESSMENT: An attractive but little-known approach and ridge walk on an attractive but little-known Munro. The scram-

bling described can easily be bypassed.

SEASONAL NOTES: When snow crests the east ridge the exposure is considerable, and the rock steps may be problematical when the bypass path is under snow. The only straightforward winter route is the west ridge.

SPELEOLOGICAL NOTE: The limestone rocks of Coire Sheilach north-west of Elleric have yielded a number of sporting caves that are among the most extensive in the area.

PATH UPDATE NOTE: New

directions are required to find the start of the path to the lost valley. The shortcut around Glenure House, shown on the sketch map, is now impassable; keep to the Land Rover tracks, as described in the updated text, to reach the bridge a couple of hundred metres beyond Glenure House. 100m further, take a side track on the right that climbs through the woods to end on open hillside. A Munro baggers' path continues but, after only 30/40m, branch right at a fork to pick up the path (indistinct at first) to the lost valley.

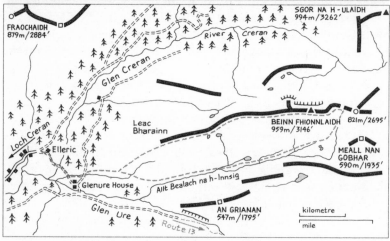

BEINN FHIONNLAIDH cannot be seen from most of the popular mountain viewpoints and is perhaps the least known Munro in the Central Highlands. Forests encroach on three sides, further dissuading access. Yet it is a fine mountain, consisting almost entirely of a single long ridge that is quite narrow near the summit and buttressed by steep, rocky flanks on each side. This route avoids the trudge up the west ridge (the Munro baggers' ascent route) to explore a far more pleasant and interesting approach.

At the head of Loch Creran on the A828, take the public road up the west side of Glen Creran and park at its end near Elleric (car park). From here, take the private road to Glenure House, then a Land Rover track that goes left into upper Glen Creran. Leave this track after only a few hundred metres, at the bridge over the first stream coming down from Beinn Fhionnlaidh, and seek out an excellent old path, indistinct at first, that crosses the southern flanks of the mountain. It begins in woods on the left-hand side of the stream and climbs high above it before crossing it and contouring into the steep-sided glen of the Allt Bealach na h-Innsig (but see Path Update Note).

The path eventually peters out in a beautiful lost valley formerly used as a summer shieling, where grassy flats offer idyllic campsites in a perfect situation. At the end of the valley, keep left to follow a side stream up to a 'lost lochan', then continue up to rejoin the main glen and reach its head, where two more lochans lie hidden on the moor to the right. From here, climb diagonally up steep grass slopes to reach the saddle between the east ridge of Beinn Fhionnlaidh and the subsidiary top given a spot height of 821m on the OS map.

The S-shaped east ridge has rocky sections and is narrow enough to give views down both sides at the same time. The crest has some short sections of enjoyable scrambling, but the easiest route requires no handwork at all. After a steep beginning the ridge bears left and levels out to the foot of the rocky final section. Two small rock bands go direct on staircases of good footholds, or a path can be used to avoid them on the left. The summit has excellent views, especially of the Glen Etive mountains.

The west ridge provides a straightforward descent. At first it rims the north face, where there are some sizeable crags and where in mist it is important not to wander out onto a spur. The ridge bears left away from here; it is broad, gentle and grassy, but with much exposed rock. Half-way down is a levelling that holds a couple of lochans, and when the ridge broadens lower down, keep left to descend to the approach track.

ROUTE 15 **SGOR NA H-ULAIDH**

	1	2	3	4	5
GRADE				X	
TERRAIN			X		
NAVIGATION			X		
SERIOUSNESS			X		

OS MAP: 41
GR: 118565
DISTANCE: 12km (7½ miles)
ASCENT: 1,100m (3,600ft)
TIME: 6½ hours

ASSESSMENT: A route of very steep slopes, high ridges and unusual views of familiar mountains on Glen Coe's 'lost' Munro. **Note:** the route is graded 4 for a short but unavoidable scramble on wet rock on the descent from Corr na Beinne; if in doubt, descend by the route of ascent, which is Grade 2.

SEASONAL NOTES: In winter, very steep snow slopes will be encountered on the ascent of both Aonach Dubh a' Ghlinne and Sgor na h-Ulaidh, and the descent via Corr na Bheinne is for experienced mountaineers only.

GET RICH QUICK NOTE: Sgor na h-Ulaidh means Peak of the Hidden Treasure.

SGOR NA H-ULAIDH is known as the 'lost' mountain of Glen Coe because it lies hidden behind a craggy outlying spur of Aonach Dubh a' Ghlinne. The ascent from any side involves very steep ground, and this gives the Sgor a truly mountainous character that makes the traverse of its summit ridges a considerable and satisfying achievement.

Begin at the bridge over the Allt na Muidhe on the A82, 3km (2 miles) east of Glen Coe village (parking 100m east of the bridge). The initial aim is to gain the top of the outlying spur of Aonach Dubh a' Ghlinne, which rises steeply ahead. Follow a

Land Rover track up the west side of the river until beyond the last buildings, then make a shallow rising traverse across the western slopes of the spur. Keep low down until you have outflanked all crags, then climb directly up steep but easy slopes of grass among rocks, gaining height fast to reach the skyline just south of the top of the spur, on the ridge leading to Sgor na h-Ulaidh.

Follow the ridge over the summit of Aonach Dubh a' Ghlinne and across a bealach to the fine summit of Stob an Fhuarain, from where ridges continue to both left and right. Take the well-worn path that descends the right-hand ridge, following the remains of an old fence to the bealach below Sgor na h-Ulaidh. On the way down you pass the small lochan after which Stob an Fhuarain is named (Peak of the Well).

Across the bealach the summit cairn of Sgor na h-Ulaidh can be seen atop the crags of Coire Dubh. The deep gash that cleaves the ridge immediately left of the summit is known as Red Gully – a formidable winter climb. The path rises steeply in tight zig-zags left of the crags to gain the summit.

If continuing round the skyline (see note in Assessment opposite), cross to the lower west top and descend to the grassy shoulder called Corr na Beinne. From here a rough path descends steep broken slopes on the right, following a broken fence. The crux of the descent is about halfway down, where the fence disappears over a greasy slab. The obvious path beside it leads onto awkward ground; a couple of easier variations will be found further right, but a short section of scrambling is unavoidable, and the rock is usually uncomfortably greasy. Care is required here.

Below the greasy slab the path veers right into the upper glen of the Allt na Muidhe. A good path is picked up on the right bank of the river and this leads back down to the Land Rover track and so to your starting point.

ROUTE 16 **CREISE and MEALL a' BHUIRIDH**

	1	2	3	4	5
GRADE				X	
TERRAIN			X		
NAVIGATION			X		
SERIOUSNESS			X		

OS MAP: 41/50
GR: 268530
DISTANCE: 13km (8 miles)
ASCENT: 1,080m (3,550ft)
TIME: 7 hours

ASSESSMENT: Easy scrambling and fine ridge walking combine to give a route of great variety and excellent views on the edge of Rannoch Moor.

SEASONAL NOTES: The summit of Creise is not easy to reach in winter. The north-east ridge of Stob a' Ghlais Choire becomes a mountaineering route, and a cornice on the eastern flanks of Creise often makes the connecting spur to Meall a' Bhuiridh difficult to reach. An ascent of Meall a' Bhuiridh via Coire Pollach remains straightforward; the main objective danger is skiers.

CAPRIC NOTE: Wild goats can sometimes be seen on the crags of Clach Leathad.

CHAIRLIFT UPDATE NOTE: Owing to warmer winters, the future of Glencoe ski area and the continued running of the chairlift is currently in doubt. Enquire at Glen Coe Visitor Centre (01855-811-307).

IT IS NOT OFTEN that a new Munro appears in Scotland, especially in the well-mapped Glen Coe area, but Creise is one such. It was elevated to Munro status during the metrication of maps in the 1970s, when it was discovered that it was higher than the Munro (Clach Leathad) of which it was formerly the north top. It is a fine mountain best reached from the north, where the north-east ridge of Stob a' Ghlais Choire provides an exciting route of ascent.

Begin at Blackrock Cottage on the White Corries ski road near the head of Glen Etive. Go west across the moor and round the end of the spur of Creag Dhubh into the Cam Ghleann; the best line crosses the flat part of the moor left of a line of telegraph poles. When viewed across the Cam Ghleann the precipitous north face of Stob a' Ghlais Choire is a daunting sight, but its left-hand edge (the north-east ridge) gives a very pleasant and surprisingly easy scramble. Walk up the glen and cross the stream to gain the foot of the ridge.

Grass slopes lead up to a short levelling and then to the foot of the rocks. After stepping onto the rock, climb diagonally right at first up a ramp, then head more or less straight up. Once over the initial steepening the angle eases then steepens again to provide more or less continuous scrambling on good rough rock among grass. Higher up, a boulderfield continues to the summit of Stob a' Ghlais Choire.

A sweeping ridge leads onwards across a saddle to Creise's flat summit ridge, then gentle slopes descend across the almost imperceptible top of Mam Coire Easain, which is really just a shoulder of Creise but was a Top until 1981. At the cliff edge on the left, look for a cairn that marks the top of the steeply descending spur leading to Meall a' Bhuiridh, but first make the short return trip to Clach Leathad for the magnificent view over the cliffs of Sron nam Forsair into Coire Ba, perhaps the largest corrie in Scotland.

The descent of the spur requires handwork but is not difficult. It leads to a beautiful, narrow U-shaped ridge that curves to the summit of Meall a' Bhuiridh. Cross to the east top for an uninterrupted view across Rannoch Moor, then return to the summit and descend the north ridge to gain the foot of the ski tows in Coire Pollach. A rough path goes down the right-hand side of the lower chairlift to the car park. Until late summer, snow in Coire Pollach may add zest to the descent, and those untroubled by their conscience should note that a chairlift may operate in summer.

ROUTE 17 THE GIANT'S STAIRCASE OF STOB BAN

	1	2	3	4	5
GRADE					X
TERRAIN					X
NAVIGATION				X	
SERIOUSNESS			X		

OS MAP: 41
GR: 252807
DISTANCE: 22km (14 miles)
ASCENT: 1,000m (3,300ft)
TIME: 8 hours

ASSESSMENT: A secret rock playground leads to the summit of a shapely but rarely seen peak. **Note:** The easiest lines reduce the grade to 4 or 3.

SEASONAL NOTES: As a rock route, the Giant's Staircase is best tackled on a hot summer's day. In winter Stob Ban is best ascended by its east or south-west ridge, but the summit snow slopes are steep whichever approach is used.

THIEVES NOTE: The Lairig Leacach (Slabby Pass) is the western end of the Thieves Road, which in clan times the men of Lochaber used as a route eastwards to plunder the fertile lands of eastern Scotland.

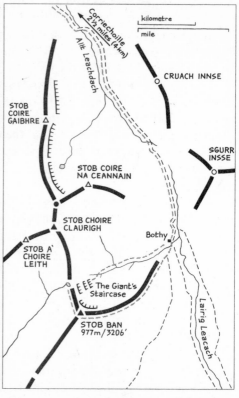

STOB BAN'S conical and retiring summit makes it one of the most alluring in the Central Highlands, and its flanks hold the additional attraction of the Giant's Staircase, a series of quartzite slabs that provide superb scrambling of all grades. The approach is as for the main range of the Grey Corries, of which Stob Ban is an outlier.

Begin at Corriechoille Farm, on the south side of the River Spean east of Spean Bridge. Take the Land Rover track that goes south up the glen of the Allt Leachdach round the eastern end of the Grey Corries. Do not begrudge the long walk-in, for it enhances the mountain's character. After 9km (5½ miles) you reach Lairig

Leacach bothy, superbly sited at the foot of Stob Ban, which towers 520m (1,700ft) overhead.

After a breather at the bothy, take the developing path along the left bank (right side) of the Allt a' Chuil Choirean, which tumbles through a fine gorge. Beyond the cascades at the head of the gorge, keep to the indistinct streamside path to cross the flat floor of Coire Claurigh and reach the foot of the Giant's Staircase at the back.

As its name implies, the staircase consists of tier upon tier of beautiful clean quartzite slabs separated by grassy terraces. The slabs are all shapes and sizes and are all set at the same tempting angle. The most direct ascent gives a hard scramble, but easy scrambling ascents using the smaller slabs are also possible, or you can avoid scrambling altogether to the left or right. The choice is yours, although it is advisable to avoid the quartzite when it is wet and slippery.

The staircase has three sections. The first section is a complex sequence of slabs that leads up to a shallow, boggy dip. Above here the second section has some fine, hard and exposed scrambling on a long rib on the right-hand side of the slabs. Above here is a rock terrace with a reedy lochan, and behind this rises the great buttress that forms the third and final section. The buttress can be turned on the right using a grassy gully, whose left-hand edge gives more excellent scrambling on a rock staircase.

You emerge on the north ridge of Stob Ban slightly above the saddle that connects it to Stob Choire Claurigh. Climb steep quartzite rubble to reach the summit, taking care not to stray too far to the left, where the slopes are exposed and dangerous. The summit is a wonderful viewpoint for the Grey Corries and the Mamores. The round continues down the east ridge, which is again steep at first, but a good path eases the going. On excellent grassy terrain, continue down the ridge all the way to the bothy and the track back to Coirechoille.

ROUTE 18 **THE TREIG TRAVERSE**

	1	2	3	4	5
GRADE	X				
TERRAIN	X				
NAVIGATION					X
SERIOUSNESS				X	

OS MAP: 41
GR: 355802
DISTANCE: 23km (14½ miles)
ASCENT: 900m (2,950ft)
TIME: 8 hours

ASSESSMENT: A short train ride into the wilderness leads to a scenic, gentle, one-way ridge walk back across two Munros.

SEASONAL NOTES: In good weather, Chno Dearg and Stob Coire Sgriodain remain straight-forward under snow except for the latter's north ridge, which gives some good winter sport. To avoid this ridge, descend into Coire an Lochain from the bealach between the two mountains.

STATION RECORD NOTE: At 410m (1,347ft) Corrour is the highest railway station in the British rail network, and the only one inaccessible by public road.

THIS IS A UNIQUE route for this book in that it is a one-way walk made possible by use of the West Highland Railway line. From Corrour Station, reached by the early morning train from Tulloch Station, the route back to Tulloch over the hills on the east side of Loch Treig is a wonderful walk that takes in two Munros and some great scenery along the way. The Munros are usually bagged from Fersit near Tulloch, but the Corrour approach is far more rewarding.

Corrour Station is an oasis in the wilderness that cannot be reached by road. When the train leaves you behind on the platform you may be forgiven for a brief moment of misgiving over what you have let yourself in for, but fear not – a path navigates the bogs to start you on your way homewards. Leave the path when it reaches the Allt Luib Ruairidh, walk under the railway bridge and head straight up the grassy slopes of Sron na Garbh-bheinne at the southern end of the east Loch Treig ridge.

The ridge rises gently on good terrain to Garbh-bheinn, where it narrows before broadening again to the summit of Meall Garbh. It gives very pleasant walking, with grand views across Loch Treig and lots of interesting erratic boulders that testify to its ice-scoured past. Beyond the second of Meall Garbh's twin tops, easy slopes continue across a bealach to the flat summit of the intriguingly named Chno Dearg (see Glossary).

Retrace your steps to the bealach and bear right across a lower bealach (very confusing in mist) to follow the ridge that forms the rim of Coire an Lochain. The ridge rises over lots of rocky knolls to the south top of Stob Coire Sgriodain, beyond which a sharp dip separates you from the main summit. The summit cairn is perched on crags overlooking fjord-like Loch Treig and offers a stunning panorama that includes not only Loch Treig but also Glen Spean and Loch Laggan.

From the summit, continue down the rocky north ridge and descend right into Coire an Lochain before reaching Sron na Garbh-bheinne. Alternatively, to add more spice to the descent, go straight over Sron na Garbh-bheinne and scramble down among rock outcrops. Once into the corrie, make for the main stream, along whose right bank a small path is developing.

At the foot of the corrie lies Fersit. From here it is less than 3km (2 miles) along the railway line to Tulloch, but as there is no path you must go by road. Do not begrudge the 6km (3½ mile) road walk, for it passes picturesque scenery (including the Inverlair kettle holes), and without it this unique expedition would not be possible.

ROUTE 19 **CARN DEARG and SGOR GAIBHRE**

	1	2	3	4	5
GRADE	X				
TERRAIN		X			
NAVIGATION			X		
SERIOUSNESS			X		

OS MAP: 42
GR: 446579
DISTANCE: 24km (15 miles)
ASCENT: 1010m (3,300ft)
TIME: 9 hours

ASSESSMENT: A scenic skyline stravaig round a great corrie, traversing two off-the-beaten-path Munros that are made accessible by good approach paths and terrain.

SEASONAL NOTES: A long route for a short winter's day, but one whose gentle gradients provide good winter walking for the suitably equipped.

TRAIN NOTE: Those who enjoy Route 18 might like to consider a similar one-way walk from Corrour Station over Carn Dearg and Sgor Gaibhre to Rannoch Station.

THE LONELY COUNTRY of the Corrour and Rannoch deer forests between Loch Ossian and Loch Ericht contains two of the most remote and least visited Munros in the Central Highlands. Unstartling in appearance and surrounded by miles of moor and bog, they are surprisingly approachable from the south, where their pleasant southern ridges enclose the vast empty spaces of Coire Eigheach.

The route begins opposite Loch Eigheach, 2¼km (1½ miles) from Rannoch Station at the end of the B846. Take the Land Rover track that crosses the moor and rises round the brow of a hill into the glen of the Allt Eigheach. Cross the river at a bridge and follow the path on the far side, which is the old track to Corrour Station and is still in excellent condition. When the path begins to level out on the slopes of Sron Leachd a' Chaorainn, climb the heathery hillside to the summit, less than 300m (1,000ft) above.

The summit marks the start of Coire Eigheach's western arm, a broad ridge that leads to Carn Dearg. Gentle gradients and short turf give pleasant walking over several intermediate tops and past a couple of small lochans, and there is plenty of time to admire the superb western panorama, across Rannoch Moor to the peaks of Glen Coe and Glen Nevis.

From the summit of Carn Dearg you can look down on Loch Ossian before turning east round the head of Coire Eigheach to cross the broad saddle of Mam Ban to Sgor Gaibhre. The gradual descent, in two stages, is followed by an equally gradual ascent to the summit of Sgor Gaibhre and a view over its steep western side to the Ben Alder group and Loch Ericht. The route then turns south along Coire Eigheach's eastern arm, undulating over a couple of small tops and down to a bealach.

Beyond the bealach a group of less well-defined tops sprawl at the mouth of the corrie and it is possible to extend the day by traversing them and making a long pathless descent to the bridge over the Allt Eigheach. Like the author, however, you will probably be content by now to descend into Coire Eigheach and pick up the excellent stalkers' path marked on the map on the far (right) bank of the river.

Note: The Allt Eigheach may become a considerable obstacle lower down so cross it as soon as possible. The path is now an all-terrain vehicle track in its upper reaches. When the wheeltracks veer away from the river, the old path continues along the bank. Both track and path give excellent walking and provide a very pleasant riverside route back down the great trench of Coire Eigheach to the approach route.

ROUTE 20 **THE ARDVERIKIE TRIO**

	1	2	3	4	5
GRADE	X				
TERRAIN		X			
NAVIGATION			X		
SERIOUSNESS	X				

OS MAP: 42
GR: 432830
DISTANCE: 25km (15½ miles)
ASCENT: 1,270m (4,150ft)
TIME: 9 hours

ASSESSMENT: A long, lonely tramp across three retiring Munros, characterised by good approach paths, rough summit terrain and great scenery.
SEASONAL NOTES: The complete route makes a long winter's day. Steep snow may be encountered on Beinn a' Chlachair, but the more gentle slopes of Geal Charn and Creag Pitridh provide good introductions to winter walking. Under snow the rough summit plateaux are sometimes easier to negotiate, but they are no place to be in foul winter weather.

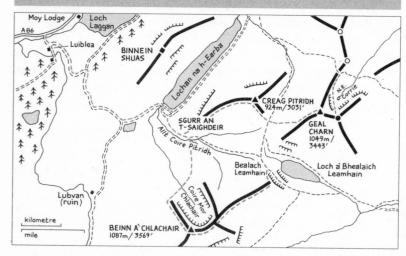

THE ARDVERIKIE FOREST (a treeless 'deer forest') is criss-crossed by a host of stalkers' paths that make its trio of reclusive Munros easy to reach. The route described here visits all features of interest on the mountains and is also (for once) the shortest way to reach the three summits.

Begin at the bridge over the River Spean on the A86 1km (½ mile) beyond the west end of Loch Laggan. Follow a Land Rover track, branching left at the first junction, right at the next and left again at the next, to reach the sandy shores of Lochan na h-Earba in the great trench behind Binnein Shuas. After crossing the bridge at the head of the loch, keep right on the main track and look for a cairn five minutes further along. This marks the start of a stalkers' path that climbs beside the Allt Coire Pitridh to the Bealach Leamhain between Beinn a' Chlachair and Geal Charn.

Follow the path until it veers left away from the stream and then make a rising traverse into the mouth of Coire Mor Chlachair, Beinn a' Chlachair's finest feature. Climb either rim of the corrie to the summit. The left-hand rim is less steep, but if you climb the right-hand rim you will avoid having to cross the rough north-east shoulder on ascent as well as descent (see below). The summit, set well back from the corrie headwall, gives panoramic views over Glen Spean.

The descent route goes down the north-east shoulder, whose boulder-strewn slopes give the mountain its name (Mountain of the Mason). Keep going until you suddenly find yourself on the brink of a great crag, with Loch a' Bhealaich Leamhain beneath your feet. Circumvent the crag on steep, broken slopes to the left to reach the stalkers' path you quit earlier.

Follow the path over the Bealach Leamhain and branch right at a fork to follow another stalkers' path up to the bealach between Geal Charn and Creag Pitridh. Leave the path at its high point to climb slopes of grass and boulders to the summit of Geal Charn. It is worth continuing beyond the summit to view the fine north-east corrie, with its inviting lochan and headwall snowbank that often lasts into summer.

Redescend to the high point of the path and cross the bealach to make the short ascent of Creag Pitridh. This conical lump of a mountain hardly seems deserving of Munro status, but it has a fine rocky top and commands wonderful views across Lochan na h-Earba. The easiest route down redescends the path from the bealach, but the more aesthetic descent route goes down Creag Pitridh's south-west ridge to the rocky eyrie of Sgurr an t-Saighdeir, before cutting left to regain the path.

ROUTE 21 **BEINN a' CHAORAINN**

	1	2	3	4	5
GRADE				X	
TERRAIN			X		
NAVIGATION			X		
SERIOUSNESS		X			

OS MAP: 34 or 41/42
GR: 400819
DISTANCE: 11km (7 miles)
ASCENT: 940m (3,100ft)
TIME: 5 /2 hours
ASSESSMENT: An easy scramble that takes a superb line up a hidden ridge between two great corries. A Central Highland minor classic.
SEASONAL NOTES: In winter the east ridge becomes a major mountaineering route with an Alpine ambience. The easier south ridge remains practicable for those comfortable on occasionally steep snow, but it can become icy when windswept.
PATH UPDATE NOTE: (1) The access path described, beginning at the bridge over the Allt na h-Uamha, is now almost impassable owing to forestry growth. Instead, it is easier to begin at the bridge over the Allt a' Chaorainn near Roughburn (GR 377814), just east of Loch Laggan dam. The upper forest track noted in the text (to which the old path was a shortcut) starts here and contours around the southern slopes of Beinn a' Chaorainn all the way to the foot of the east ridge. (2) Instead of descending the south ridge, go down the broad south-west ridge, staying right of Meall Clachaig to find the Munro baggers' approach path back to Roughburn. The sketch map shows the South Top as the summit and the Centre Top as a Top. As noted in the updated text, this situation has now been reversed.

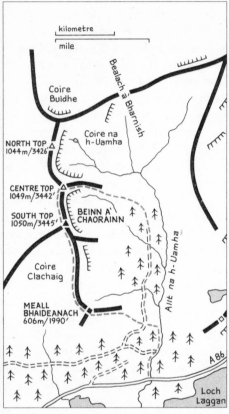

THE TRIPLE-TOPPED plateau summit of Beinn a' Chaorainn looks dull from the roadside but, like its Glen Spean neighbour Creag Meagaidh, the mountain's east face harbours some magnificent hidden corries. The three tops are almost equally high and this has proved problematical for mapmakers over the years. For most of the last century the South Top was considered the highest, but in the 1970s resurveying made the Centre Top the highest. The latest surveys give both Tops the same height in metres, but the Centre Top is still considered to be slightly higher.

Such matters are, of course, irrelevant to *Classic Routes* connoisseurs, who will find rearing skywards between the two great eastern corries the superb east ridge, where an easy scramble in spectacular situations provides a route to the plateau that has a real mountaineering flavour.

Begin on the A86 in Glen Spean about 5km (3 miles) west of Loch Laggan, at the bridge over the Allt na h-Uamha. Go through the gate in the fence on the left-hand side of the bridge and follow an overgrown path through the forestry plantation on the west bank of the river. The path passes the end of a forest track and reaches a forest fence, where it bears left to reach an upper forest track (but see Path Update Note 1). Follow this latter track through another plantation of trees to the upper forest fence, then go left across gently rising moorland to the foot of the east ridge.

Initial steep heathery slopes lead up to a levelling, above which the ridge proper rears in rocky splendour between its two flanking corries. It consists of a series of rock steps that begins easily, becomes harder in the middle and then eases off again towards the top. The line of least resistance is never more than an easy scramble, but there are harder lines aplenty and even the easiest route has some degree of exposure in places. There are some superb situations and the rock is excellent, with fault lines tilted up towards you at a perfect angle to provide good steps and holds that the fingers curl around easily.

The summit (Centre Top) is directly at the top of the ridge and comes much too soon. The North Top lies a short distance away across a shallow dip and the stroll to it round the rim of Coire na h-Uamha makes a pleasant add-on return trip with spacious northern views. From the Centre Top cross another dip to gain the South Top, then continue down the grass and stones of the broad south ridge, facing magnificent views across Glen Spean to Loch Treig. At the foot of the south ridge it is worth continuing over the lowly top of Meall Bhaideanach for the view along Loch Laggan before rejoining the path back down to your starting point (but see Path Update Note 2).

The
Western Highlands

ROUTE 22 **BEINN RESIPOL**

	1 2 3 4 5
GRADE	X
TERRAIN	X
NAVIGATION	X
SERIOUSNESS	X

OS MAP: 40
GR: 818638
DISTANCE: 13km (8 miles)
ASCENT: 810m (2,650ft)
TIME: 5 hours

ASSESSMENT: An historic path leads to rugged summit slopes and breathtaking views on an easy West coast Corbett.

SEASONAL NOTES: Normally no especial difficulties in winter. The summit ridge and easy (if fairly steep) snow slopes above Meall an t-Slugain provide a good introduction to the demands of Scottish winter walking.

WELL NOTE: On the Bealach nan Carn some amusement can be had searching for St Finnan's Well at GR 798655.

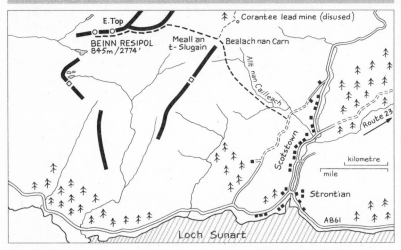

THE DISTRICTS OF Ardgour and Sunart west of Fort William are devoid of Munros but full of rugged mountains characterised by wonderful ridge walking and superb views. Rocky Garbh Bheinn is described in Route 31 in *100 Best Routes*, but this further volume of walks offers a chance to explore three more fine routes (Routes 22-24) off the beaten track.

Sunart is completely dominated by the extensive mountain mass of Beinn Resipol, whose rugged topography is masked on most sides by a skirt of moorland. Only when seen from the west does the attractive summit cone give some idea of the true nature of the mountain and the vast panorama that awaits those who reach the top.

The most pleasant ascent starts in the east and leaves the western vista to burst into view at the last moment. The start of the route is found by leaving the A861 at Strontian, driving north for two miles on the Scotstown road and branching left on a minor road a few hundred metres past the last house. Park at the gate at the road end and follow the continuing Land Rover track to a fork beside a tree. Branch right here on a track that doubles back to make a pleasant ascent of the shallow valley of the Allt nan Cailleach.

You are now on the historic miners' track that crosses spacious moorland to the eighteenth century Corantee lead mine. Beinn Resipol remains hidden until you reach the crest of the moor at the Bealach nan Carn, where a host of scattered cairns testifies to the route's even earlier use as a 'coffin route' to the sacred burial isle of St Finnan in Loch Shiel; the cairns mark spots where funeral processions rested.

Leave the path when it bears right to descend to the old mine, cut across the moor to Meall an t-Slugain at the foot of Beinn Resipol's upper slopes and then head for the skyline. The ascent is longer than it looks but grassy terrain makes the going easy; those wishing a spot of scrambling will find much exposed rock, especially on the right. Higher up, you arrive at a levelling, and from here on the ridge narrows to provide wonderful walking up to the rocky east top and across a long saddle to the summit, with Loch Sunart on one side and Loch Shiel on the other.

When the summit cairn finally arrives it feels almost exposed, as the western slopes of the mountain drop away steeply to reveal a seascape that is simply immense. When you have drunk your fill of this magical spot, return to your starting point by the route of ascent.

ROUTE 23 **SGURR DHOMHNUILL**

	1	2	3	4	5
GRADE			X		
TERRAIN		X			
NAVIGATION				X	
SERIOUSNESS		X			

OS MAP: 40
GR: 825633
DISTANCE: 18km (11½ miles)
ASCENT: 1,160m (3,800ft)
TIME: 8 hours

ASSESSMENT: A rugged ridge walk through a fascinating landscape. Interesting features visited include an oak forest, old lead mines and one of the best collections of erratic boulders in the Highlands.

SEASONAL NOTES: The extremely steep grassy hillsides of Sgurr Dhomhnuill can be treacherous under snow and dangerously slippery when wet.

MINING NOTE: Lead was mined at Strontian from 1722 to 1872. The mineral strontianite was first found here in 1764 and this led to the isolation of the element strontium in 1790.

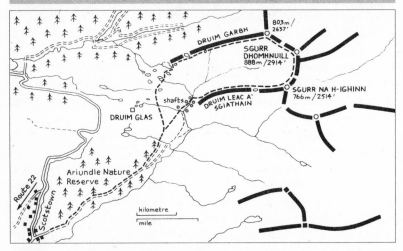

SGURR DHOMHNUILL is the highest and most shapely peak in Ardgour, yet it remains relatively little known. Its very steep, conical summit supports a number of ridges, two of which enclose a deep western glen to provide an entertaining circular ridge walk that passes a number of interesting features rarely seen to such perfection on Scottish mountains.

To reach the car park at the start of the route, leave the A861 at Strontian, drive north for one mile on the Scotstown road and then branch right into Ariundle Nature Reserve. Walk along a continuing Land Rover track through serene broad-leaved woodland, keep left at a fork and reach the forest boundary after 4km (2¼ miles). An historic miners' track continues to the eighteenth century Fee Donald lead mine workings in a surprisingly green and picturesque spot at the foot of the two ridges. A cairn on a boulder marks the end of the track, where an old shaft on the left can be explored with the aid of a torch.

Cross the stream and climb directly to the rugged crest of Druim Leac a' Sgiathain, where many exposed ribs of rough granite beg to be clambered upon. The complex ridge undulates over a series of knolls as it rises pleasantly to the foot of the pyramid summit of Sgurr na h-Ighinn, which can be climbed easily on grass or scrambled up on outcrops.

Easier slopes of grass and broken rock then descend to a bealach, above which the two-tiered upper slopes of Sgurr Dhomhnuill rise steeply overhead. The second tier begins with some sizeable crags, but these are easily outflanked by a steep little path on the right. As befits the highest mountain in the region, there is a considerable summit view.

The descent of the far side looks dramatically steep, but on closer inspection there are traces of a path on the left and it is possible to make a way down steep grass among outcrops with only minimal use of the nether regions. After you have tumbled onto the bealach at the bottom there are several possible ways onward up easier slopes to Druim Garbh, a fine ridge whose undulations are followed westwards parallel to Druim Leac a' Sgiathain.

From the dip on the ridge, just before the first lochan shown on the map, it is possible to descend to the miners' track, but those with energy remaining should on no account miss the continuing ridge, which boasts a remarkable series of beautiful ridge-top lochans and erratic boulders. Good route-finding is needed, but this only adds to the fun and it is worth continuing at least until the ridge degenerates into a moorland plateau before heading down to the forest boundary to rejoin the outward route.

ROUTE 24 **SGURR GHIUBHSACHAIN**

	1	2	3	4	5
GRADE				X	
TERRAIN				X	
NAVIGATION					X
SERIOUSNESS			X		

OS MAP: 40
GR: 924794
DISTANCE: 17km (10½ miles)
ASCENT: 1,110m (3,650ft)
TIME: 8 hours

ASSESSMENT: An entertaining rocky ridge in scenic country gives plenty of opportunities to indulge scrambling and routefinding skills.

SEASONAL NOTES: A serious winter route on mixed snow and rock, with some steep and exposed situations.

SCENIC NOTE: With a length of 29km (18 miles), Loch Shiel is one of the longest and narrowest lochs in Scotland. It was at Glenfinnan at its head that Bonnie Prince Charlie raised his standard in 1745, and in the classic view along the loch from the commemorative monument, Sgurr Ghiubhsachain is one of the two framing peaks.

ALTHOUGH THERE ARE no Munros on the south side of the A830 Fort William-Mallaig road, a brace of craggy Corbetts on the east side of Loch Shiel provides a sporting diversion high above the lochside on a hot summer's day. Begin 2½km (1½ miles) east of Glenfinnan, where a Land Rover track crosses the Callop River and bears right to follow the eastern shore of Loch Shiel.

Follow the track down the lochside as far as Geusachan cottage, above which the north-east ridge of Sgurr Ghiubhsachain, the first Corbett, forms an appealing line. From the cottage, cross rough ground to gain the crest of the ridge, where traces of a path ease the ascent of the steep lower slopes of grass and heather. With height the ridge gains in interest, sporting an increasing number of small tarns and becoming much rockier (although almost all scrambling can be avoided if you wish).

The first real obstacle is an arrowhead-shaped crag, where easy scrambling will be found right of the crest. Higher up, the developing path bypasses a harder crag, and then any further problems can be avoided on the right to reach the summit of Meall a' Choire Chruinn, from where there are stunning views up and down Loch Shiel.

With better terrain underfoot, continue across a complex saddle and climb the steep upper slopes of Sgurr Ghiubhsachain through a tangle of crags. Bypass the obvious main crag on the right, then work back up to the crest, which narrows pleasantly to the north top of Sgurr Ghiubhsachain and across a dip to the main summit.

To outflank hidden crags that complicate the direct descent to the saddle below Sgorr Craobh a' Chaorainn, the second Corbett, return to the dip between Sgurr Ghiubhsachain's two tops before descending. From the saddle a gentle grassy ridge climbs to Sgorr Craobh a' Chaorainn's surprising summit, a rock 'astrodome' beneath which you will pause for some time before deciding whether to tackle it to the left or right.

The walk above Loch Shiel can be prolonged by continuing along the ridge to Sgorr nan Cearc, but the most pleasant route back, avoiding a moorland crossing, goes down Sgorr Craobh a' Chaorainn's north-east ridge. The ridge descends steeply to a broad saddle, crosses the large pimple of Meall na Cuartaige and narrows pleasantly for a final, gentle descent to the path down the Callop Glen.

The path along the glen has seen better days and can become quite boggy, but it still provides a fast descent beside fine mixed woodland and the rushing Allt na Cruaiche. Bypass the house at Callop on a riverbank path that joins a Land Rover track and leads back to your starting point.

ROUTE 25 **GULVAIN**

	1	2	3	4	5
GRADE		X			
TERRAIN	X				
NAVIGATION	X				
SERIOUSNESS		X			

OS MAP: 40/41
GR: 961794
DISTANCE: 21km (13 miles)
ASCENT: 1,080m (3,550ft)
TIME: 8 hours
ASSESSMENT: A straightforward but relentless ascent leads to a wonderful sky-touching ridge walk.

SEASONAL NOTES: The steepness of Gulvain's slopes under snow should not be underestimated, especially on descent. Although normally of no technical difficulty, the summit ridge is capable of being wind-sculpted into a great variety of complex snow forms. A slip on either side would result in a descent to the glen in record time (certificate awarded posthumously).

ARTISTIC NOTE: Coire Screamhach contains a soft rock that local shepherds used to carve into ornaments.

GULVAIN IS A GREAT isolated hulk of a mountain that is the most easterly Munro in the Locheil district north of the Fort William-Mallaig road. It is well hidden from the roadside at the end of curving Gleann Fionnlighe and, as if to confuse prospective summiteers further, it has two tops, of which the first carries the trig pillar but the second is higher and hidden away on another map. As if that weren't enough, the mountain even has two names, Gaor Bheinn being its pseudonym.

You may be forgiven for thinking that Gulvain wishes to remain inviolate, a view that will be reinforced by the first sight of its infamously steep guarding slopes. In the event the ascent is indeed steep but nowhere difficult, and those who tackle it will be rewarded for their endeavours by a wonderful ridge walk.

The route begins opposite the junction of the A830 and the A861 at the west end of Loch Eil. Drive up to the houses and turn right across a bridge, where there are parking spaces. A Land Rover track runs from here up Gleann Fionnlighe, first on the east side and then on the west, passing the cottage at Wauchan and continuing in an unmaintained state almost to the Allt a' Choire Reidh at the foot of Gulvain.

A path continues across the river (bridge) to a fork. Take the left branch straight up Gulvain's steep grassy southern slopes. There is no respite for 730m (2,400ft), until a minor top is reached at 855m (2,805ft), and there are no views to distract from the task in hand owing to the convex nature of the slope and the flanking hills on each side. Higher up, the path becomes indistinct and intermittent, but the going remains excellent and cannot be used as an excuse for the length of time the ascent seems to be taking.

At the minor top the twin summits of Gulvain come into view at last and the first of them (the south top) is soon underfoot. The beautiful summit ridge twists its way onwards across an intervening dip to the higher north top and summit. The slopes on either side drop away steeply, and owing to the mountain's isolation there is a feeling of great height; on ascent from the dip there is one section that is invigoratingly narrow. On no account fail to go a couple of hundred metres beyond the summit to the edge of Coire Screamhach, a great rocky hollow gouged out of the north side of the mountain, from where there is a good view of Loch Arkaig.

The return route reverses the outward route, giving you time to ponder: was it worth it? Do eagles fly?

ROUTE 26 **SGURR NA H-AIDE**

	1	2	3	4	5
GRADE				X	
TERRAIN					X
NAVIGATION					X
SERIOUSNESS					X

OS MAP: 33 or 40
GR: 988916
DISTANCE: 23km (14½ miles)
ASCENT: 990m (3,250ft)
TIME: 9 hours

ASSESSMENT: An entertainingly complex and rugged ridge leads to a couple of easy scrambles on the bold twin peaks of an unjustly ignored Corbett.

SEASONAL NOTES:
A lengthy winter route but one that has little technical difficulty apart from the scrambles on the twin summits. The day can be shortened by use of A' Chuil bothy on the south side of Glen Dessarry.

TOPONYMIC NOTE: Sgurr na h-Aide is named after its shape, and means Hat Peak.

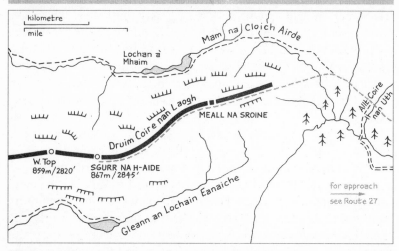

SGURR NA H-AIDE is an attractive conical peak at the head of Glen Dessarry that makes a perfect partner for Sgurr na Ciche across the glen (Route 35 in *100 Best Routes*). It commands a superb position between two of the most picturesque passes in the Highlands, Gleann an Lochain Eanaiche and Mam na Cloich Airde, while to the west it throws out a long ridge that continues for some miles between Loch Nevis and Loch Morar. Only from the east is access easy, via a rugged, undulating ridge (Druim Coire nan Laogh) whose countless rocky knolls, hidden lochans and final scramble give the mountain great character.

The approach along Glen Dessarry is as for Sgurr na Ciche. From the road end at Loch Arkaig west of Spean Bridge, take the Land Rover track past Glendessarry Farm to Upper Glendessarry Cottage. When you reach the fence round the cottage, go over the stile on the right to pick up the path that continues along the glen above forestry plantations. Follow the path past the Allt Coire nan Uth to the upper edge of the trees, then cross the glen to the foot of the rocky western shoulder of Sgurr na h-Aide, called Meall na Sroine.

Note that the Allt Coire nan Uth can also be reached by mountain bike along a forest track on the south side of Glen Dessarry; this ends at a bridge across the River Dessarry from where a path climbs beside the Allt Coire nan Uth to join the main path.

Climb Meall na Sroine direct; it is a rough ascent on long grass and the less said about it the better. The complex, slabby top lies a short distance over the skyline and marks the start of the ridge walk along Druim Coire nan Laogh. Soon Sgurr na h-Aide's twin conical summits come into glorious view across a lovely lochan as the ridge narrows and heads westwards between its two deep, flanking glens.

The terrain is incredibly complex, forcing you to weave to and fro as you clamber over and round the rocky knolls. Another large lochan is passed as the ascent steepens and before long you are faced by the summit buttress, negotiated by an easy, earthy scramble.

The return trip to the lower west top is not included in the route timing but is recommended for an uninterrupted view westwards to the sea. The final section of the ascent again involves an easy scramble – add 1½ km (1 mile), 120m (400ft) and 1 hour for the return trip. At least go beyond the summit to the top of the next rise to see the whole of mighty Loch Morar at your feet. Return to your starting point by the route of ascent.

ROUTE 27 **SGURR NAN COIREACHAN**

	1	2	3	4	5
GRADE			X		
TERRAIN			X		
NAVIGATION				X	
SERIOUSNESS			X		

OS MAP: 33 or 40
GR: 988916
DISTANCE: 18 km (11½ miles)
ASCENT: 1,250m (4,100ft)
TIME: 8 hours

ASSESSMENT: A narrow, enjoyable and rarely-done ridge walk leads across three lower tops to the beautiful roof-like summit ridges of a rocky Munro.

SEASONAL NOTES: A sporting winter route for budding Alpinists. The traverse from Druim a' Chuirn to Sgurr Cos na Breachd-laoidh and the rib leading up to Sgurr nan Coireachan give the most technical problems, but the steep descents from Sgurr Cos na Breachd-laoidh and Sgurr nan Coireachan also need care, as a slip would deposit you in the glen sooner than anticipated.

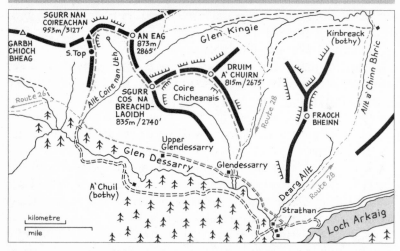

RUGGED SGURR NAN COIREACHAN is one of four Munros that lie on the long ridge separating Glen Dessarry from Loch Quoich. Its fine roof-like summit ridges are usually reached by an ascent of the penitentially steep south ridge or during a traverse of the other Munros, but the most interesting approach crosses three lower tops and includes a seldomly traversed, entertaining little ridge.

Begin at Loch Arkaig road end, west of Spean Bridge, and walk up the Glen Dessarry track as far as the stream that comes down to the right of Druim a' Chuirn. Take the path up the right bank (left side) of this stream as far as the foot of Druim a' Chuirn's grassy south-west ridge, then climb the steadily rising ridge all the way to the summit.

There are two tops of about equal height; the summit cairn crowns the first and beyond it the terrain becomes rockier. At the second top the ridge bears left and becomes pleasantly narrow as it crosses a bealach to Sgurr Cos na Breachd-laoidh. A spot of handwork is required if you follow the broken fence along the rocky crest. On the bealach there is broken rock 'castle' (easily bypassed).

From the summit of Sgurr Cos na Breachd-laoidh slopes of rock and grass drop steeply in two tiers to a bealach and rise more steadily to the summit of An Eag, a minor top on the main ridge between Sgurr Mor and Sgurr nan Coireachan. Sgurr Mor is best climbed by Route 28.

The ridge to Sgurr nan Coireachan takes the form of a steep rib that is flanked by crags on the right. A path climbs the rib left of the crest; occasional handwork is required but there is surprisingly little exposure unless you go further right in search of more exciting ways up. At the top of the rib a short stroll along the beautiful summit ridge leads to the summit, from where there are superb views of the Loch Quoich mountains and westwards to Loch Nevis. Ahead on the main ridge lie Garbh Chioch Mhor and Sgurr na Ciche, but these are perhaps best left for another day (see Route 35 in *100 Best Routes*).

To descend, go southwards down a developing path that is the Munro baggers' ascent route. After an initial steep descent from the rocky summit, stroll out along another fine ridge to the south top then continue down relentlessly steep grass slopes among crags (while giving thanks to the author for helping you avoid this route as a way up!). At the bottom you will meet the path along Glen Dessarry, which at Upper Glendessarry cottage becomes a Land Rover track that leads back to your starting point.

ROUTE 28 **SGURR MOR**

	1	2	3	4	5
GRADE	X				
TERRAIN	X				
NAVIGATION			X		
SERIOUSNESS				X	

OS MAP: 33
GR: 988916
DISTANCE: 24km (15 miles)
ASCENT: 1,650m (5,400ft)
TIME: 9½ hours

ASSESSMENT: A long day's tramp through remote country to a scenic ridge that traverses a massive Munro and its graceful neighbour.

SEASONAL NOTES: A long winter route when stalkers' paths are obliterated by snow, but one that can be broken at Kinbreack bothy. Under snow the steep slopes of Sgurr Mor seem even steeper and exposure more pronounced. The craggy south-west ridge may prove particularly awkward. When swollen with snowmelt, the River Kingie may prove an additional obstacle.

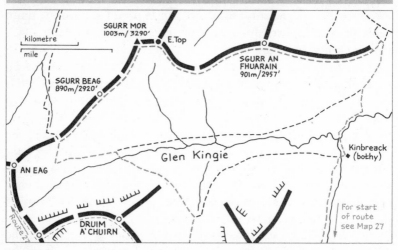

SGURR MOR'S BULKY shape and predominantly grassy slopes make it the least immediately appealing of the four Munros on the north side of Glen Dessarry, and it is also the most difficult to reach. It is a superb viewpoint, however, and when approached by the graceful ridges of its shapely neighbour Sgurr an Fhuarain and the selection of good stalkers' paths described here, it gives a rewarding route.

The key to the ascent is Glen Kingie at the foot of the two peaks, and the shortest route to here is from Loch Arkaig road end, west of Spean Bridge. Fraoch Bheinn stands between Loch Arkaig and Glen Kingie but a route round the mountain is made easy by two stalkers' paths that cross the bealachs on each side of it.

From the road end, walk up the Glen Dessarry track to the Dearg Allt, the first major stream on the right, then climb the path up its left (near) bank, beginning at a cairn 50m before the stream. Higher up, when the path becomes intermittent, follow the stream up onto the broad grassy bealach. Pick up another path that descends the far side beside the Allt a' Chinn Bhric to Kinbreack bothy in the wilds of Glen Kingie.

Beyond the bothy, follow the indistinct path down to the River Kingie and ford it (normally easy). Go right along the far bank until you reach an old fence. About 100m further along, at a fork at a ruined gate, go left on a path that climbs to another path higher up the hillside. Follow this path to the foot of the east ridge of Sgurr an Fhuarain and climb the well-defined, grassy ridge direct. The summit affords good views over the Loch Quoich mountains and a fine prospect of Sgurr Mor, which from here appears as a massive cone towering over a slabby east face.

The beautifully proportioned connecting ridge to Sgurr Mor gives a fine high-level stroll, and the 300m (1,000ft) ascent to the east top is eased by a zigzagging stalkers' path that will be with you all the way back down to Glen Kingie. From the east top a short stroll leads to the main summit and a fine view of the ridge ahead as it twists its way westwards over Sgurr nan Coireachan (Route 27).

Keep to the path as it wends its way down the craggy south-west ridge and over the steep lump of Sgurr Beag to the bealach below An Eag. At the far end of the bealach the path rises left across the ridge and descends into upper Glen Kingie. When the path approaches its closest point to the River Kingie, make a rising traverse right onto the bealach west of Fraoch Bheinn and pick up a good path that descends to Glendessarry and the track back to your starting point.

ROUTE 29 **MEALL NA TEANGA**

	1	2	3	4	5
GRADE		X			
TERRAIN	X				
NAVIGATION				X	
SERIOUSNESS		X			

OS MAP: 34
GR: 271952
DISTANCE: 16km (10 miles)
ASCENT: 1,100m (3,600ft)
TIME: 7 hours

ASSESSMENT: An unconventional route, for experienced hillwalkers, to the summit of a Great Glen Munro, with soaring ridges, hidden corries, glorious views and terrain that's a joy to walk on.

SEASONAL NOTES: In winter, very steep snow slopes guard all sides of Meall na Teanga. The direct ascent from the Cam Bhealach is the most feasible approach, but even here the slope is steep and broken. At its finest, the connecting ridge to Meall Coire Lochain is a corniced snow arête – beautiful but difficult.

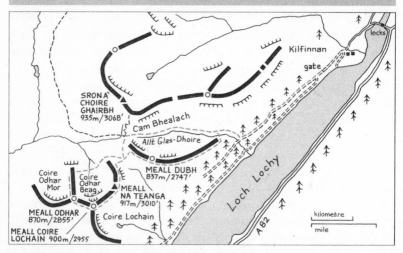

Meall na Teanga and Sron a' Choire Ghairbh, the only two Munros in the Great Glen, tower over the west side of Loch Lochy and provide commanding views, but detailed study of the map is required if an optimal route is to be found around their finest corries and ridges.

The most interesting approach begins at a locked gate on the forest road 1km (½ mile) south of Kilfinnan at the north end of Loch Lochy. Keep right at a fork after a few hundred metres and follow the road to the Allt Glas-Dhoire. A beautiful path, almost

Alpine in character, branches right 80m before the stream to climb through a tree-lined gorge into a gracefully curving upper glen.

At the head of the glen is the Cam Bhealach between Meall na Teanga and Sron a' Choire Ghairbh. From here a detour can be made up a zigzagging stalkers' path to the summit of Sron a' Choire Ghairbh – add 2½km (1½ miles), 325m (1,070ft) of ascent and 1½ hours for the return trip.

To reach Meall na Teanga from the Cam Bhealach, first climb steep grass slopes to the bealach between the summit and Meall Dubh. The summit now lies directly above, but a more interesting ascent route traverses steep grass slopes round the mountain's northern flank into the perfectly proportioned grassy bowl of Coire Odhar Beag, one of two great northern corries. Climb the grassy slopes on the far side of the corrie to gain the ridge that separates it from its neighbour, Coire Odhar Mor.

With very pleasant short turf underfoot, follow the ridge to the top of Meall Odhar and then round the head of Coire Odhar Beag to the top of Meall Coire Lochain, with great views of Ben Nevis and along the Great Glen. The ridge then becomes more exciting as it continues narrowly round the corrie rim to the summit of Meall na Teanga. The first section is almost a knife edge, but there is a good path and no difficulty.

From the summit ridge of Meall na Teanga, steep slopes descend to the bealach below Meall Dubh. Detour left to avoid crags then stay close to the edge until you can see a way down. From the bealach the easiest return route is via the Cam Bhealach, but an attractive alternative beckons.

By climbing Meall Dubh and walking out along its fine north-east ridge, you will obtain sublime views of the Great Glen, with the whole of Loch Lochy beneath your feet. You pay for this, lower down, by having to negotiate a band of broken crags, steep heather and the awkward gorge of the Allt Glas-Dhoire to regain the path above the trees. Decision time!

ROUTE 30 **THE DRUIM CHOSAIDH**

	1 2 3 4 5
GRADE	X
TERRAIN	X
NAVIGATION	X
SERIOUSNESS	X

OS MAP: 33
GR: 985036
DISTANCE: 26km (16½ miles)
ASCENT: 960m (3,150ft)
TIME: 11 hours

ASSESSMENT: A rough lochside approach walk into Knoydart's rugged heartland leads to a lengthy ridge walk that becomes increasingly exciting as it progresses.

SEASONAL NOTES: A long winter's day that gives good sport. The ascent of the second top on the final notched section of ridge requires special care.

CHARLIE NOTE: Do not follow in the footsteps of Bonnie Prince Charlie, who slipped on Meall an Spardain and was saved only by a small bush.

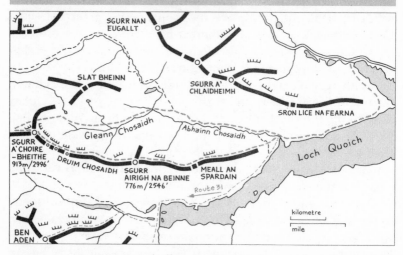

ROUTES 30 AND 31 are challenging routes that explore the magnificently untamed country around the western reaches of Loch Quoich. The mountains here are remote, rugged, exciting and guarded by long, mostly pathless approaches. The Druim Chosaidh is one metre short of Munro status and is rarely visited, but it gives the best ridge walk in Knoydart.

The expletive-inducing lochside approach walk begins on the Kinlochhourn road at the head of the north-west arm of Loch Quoich. Cross the river that flows into the loch (using stepping stones or a dubious old bridge just upstream) and follow the shore. Stay high (about 50m) above shoreline mudflats as far as the point below Sron Lice na Fearna, then choose your own route along the rocky shore or through tussocky grass above it.

After 5km (3 miles) and about 2 hours the Abhainn Chosaidh is reached. Cross or ford the river and climb straight up the grassy hillside ahead. When the angle eases, the ridge walk along the Druim Chosaidh begins, with lots of entertaining rocky slabs, knolls and hollows (Druim Chosaidh means Ridge of Nooks). The ridge crosses Meall an Spardain and undulates down to a bealach, beyond which slabs of rock festoon the ascent to Sgurr Airigh na Beinne. From the summit you get your first view of the route's climax – the dramatic final section of ridge leading up to the highpoint of Sgurr a' Choire-bheithe.

The descent to the next bealach crosses two sharp tops that are easier than they look, although you will probably use hands on the rocky descent from the second. Easier slopes re-ascend to a pleasant level section that gives you time (too much time!) to contemplate the intimidating, notched final section of ridge ahead. There are four tops, of which the last is the summit of Sgurr a' Choire-bheithe.

The first top is a grassy walk – then the fun starts. The second top gives a vegetated scramble with some exposure; there are some good hand and foot holds and the author also managed to find a couple of useful knee holds. Once up, follow the narrow and rocky ridge to the third top, an imposing pinnacle that yields to a surprisingly easy scramble on large blocks of rock. Easier slopes then continue to the summit for stunning views of Loch Hourn below, and its surrounding peaks.

The descent goes northwards but, to avoid an initial very steep section, first continue down the pleasant west ridge to just before a minor top and cut back below the upper slopes. Make for the lochan at GR 905022, cross a low bealach into Gleann Chosaidh and follow the glen down to a welcome path that takes you most of the way back down to Loch Quoich. It seems a long way back to the road.

ROUTE 31 **BEN ADEN**

	1	2	3	4	5
GRADE				X	
TERRAIN					X
NAVIGATION					X
SERIOUSNESS					X

OS MAP: 33
GR: 985036
DISTANCE: 29km (18 miles)
ASCENT: 1,000m (3,300ft)
TIME: 11 hours

ASSESSMENT: An even longer lochside approach walk than Route 30 leads to an enjoyable and scenic scramble on a perfect miniature mountain.

SEASONAL NOTES: A long route for a short winter's day. Lochside snow can hamper or ease the approach walk, depending on its consistency. When the rocks are iced or when snow lies on the steeper sections, Ben Aden's east-north-east ridge should be attempted by experienced mountaineers only. It is also best avoided when wet.

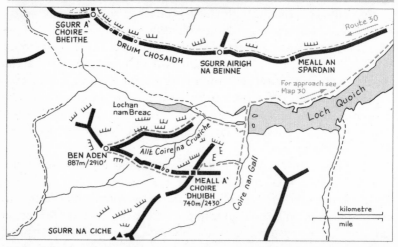

THE FAR WESTERN reaches of Loch Quoich have a remote and rough-hewn splendour that makes any trip here something out of the ordinary. The most attractive mountain in the area is shapely Ben Aden, a quintessentially rugged Knoydart peak whose scenic east-north-east ridge provides a superb ascent with a real mountaineering flavour, on granite pegmatite that is a joy to come to grips with.

The lengthy lochside approach follows Route 30 as far as the Abhainn Chosaidh and then takes to a marshy but welcome old track that continues to the two small dams at the end of the loch (10km/6 miles, about 3½ hours). Beyond the second dam, take the continuing path that goes left round a hillock, then branch right on another path that climbs over into the glen leading up to wild and beautiful Lochan nam Breac. The path crosses the Allt Coire na Cruaiche and reaches a small bealach above the lochan.

The ascent begins here (at last!), on steep slopes of rough grass that climb to a more well-defined ridge. Height is gained fast and you soon find yourself on magnificent easy-angled slabs of rough granite. As you continue upwards the ridge steepens and narrows, but have faith that no matter how problematic the route ahead may seem, a hidden passage of delightfully easy scrambling will be playfully revealed at the last moment.

At about 700m (2,300ft) the ridge swings left and at about 750m (2,450ft) you arrive at a huge flat slab of rock. Follow the end of the slab to the left of the ridge, then climb a bouldery slope back over to the right to find the easiest continuation. The ridge continues narrow for a while, crosses a small dip and then surmounts a rock tower, which can be taken direct or bypassed on the left. Above here, easier slopes lead to the summit and wonderful views of the mountains of the Knoydart peninsula sandwiched between Lochs Hourn and Nevis.

To vary the descent route, return to the dip in the ridge and descend right, steeply among crags, to a bealach. From here a broad, rugged ridge continues to Meall a' Choire Dhuibh, whose summit is the leftmost of several tops. The key to the descent from here is an old stalker's path that descends into Coire nan Gall. To find it, wend your way down among crags to a levelling on the north-west ridge, then cut back right into a corrie and descend steep grass slopes on the right of the stream until you come across the path. The path is overgrown and marshy but it is worth seeking out. It leads back to the dam and the simple matter of the 10km (6 mile) walk out.

ROUTE 32 **GAIRICH**

	1 2 3 4 5
GRADE	X
TERRAIN	X
NAVIGATION	X
SERIOUSNESS	X

OS MAP: 33
GR: 070025
DISTANCE: 16km (10 miles)
ASCENT: 810 m (2,650ft)
TIME: 5½ hours

ASSESSMENT: A gentle approach leads to an exciting ridge walk on an eyrie above Loch Quoich.

SEASONAL NOTES: In winter the ascent of the east ridge involves the negotiation of steep, exposed snow slopes, and iced rock may increase the difficulties.

HYDROLOGICAL NOTE: The truncated path network around Loch Quoich is the result of the enlargement of the original loch to form a reservoir. The raising of the water level by 30m (100ft) also submerged the cottages at Kinlochquoich at the foot of Ben Aden.

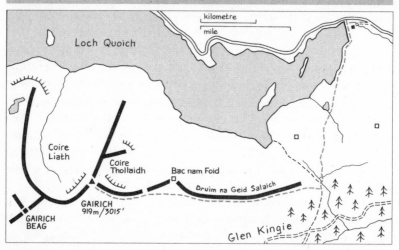

The isolated, shapely peak of Gairich makes an attractive back-drop to the view westwards along the Kinlochhourn road. Loch Quoich curls round the foot of the mountain and the dam at the eastern end offers an obvious approach route, somewhat boggy at first but developing into an exciting ascent of the east ridge. From the shores of the loch the ridge can be seen curving its way skywards round the rim of craggy Coire Thollaidh and, if this is not enticement enough, the view from the summit will be all you would expect from such a finely situated mountain.

The route begins at the dam. Cross to the far side and follow the stony shore, or an extremely boggy path just above it, for about 600m. Here you join an old stalker's path that was built before the enlargement of the loch. It emerges from the water and climbs away from the lochside, past reedy Lochan an Fhigheadair and onto the crest of a low moor, from where it descends to join another path at the edge of forestry plantations in lower Glen Kingie.

Bear left along this new path for about 100m, to the top of the rise in front of you, then fork right on an overgrown path that leads back up to the forest fence. Here the overgrown path becomes another excellent stalker's path that climbs onto the gently rising ridge of Druim na Geid Salaich.

When the stalker's path ends at a cairn, follow the line of a continuing boggy path up the broad ridge and onto the rolling plateau at the foot of Gairich's steep summit pyramid (it is best to keep left of the rounded top of Bac nam Foid to avoid the peaty saddle beyond). The path then improves again as it makes a rising traverse well left of Coire Thollaidh before zigzagging steeply back up among outcrops to the crest of the east ridge at the corrie rim.

The ridge becomes quite narrow above steep drops as it rises to a rock band that cannot be outflanked; this yields easily to a short scramble, fortunately on the non-exposed side, that gives the route its grading of 4. Above, easier slopes continue to the roof-like summit and immense views over Loch Quoich. The best views are obtained from the rim of Coire Liath, a few hundred metres beyond the cairn, and you will want to spend some time here.

The return route reverses the route of ascent, but for once this is no hardship. The rock band is perhaps best negotiated facing outwards if wearing a rucksack, the Druim na Geid Salaich is a very pleasant stroll and even the moorland crossing doesn't seem so bad on the way back.

ROUTE 33 **SGURR A' MHAORAICH**

	1	2	3	4	5
GRADE			X		
TERRAIN				X	
NAVIGATION			X		
SERIOUSNESS	X				

OS MAP: 33
GR: 010035
DISTANCE: 14km (8½ miles)
ASCENT: 1,030m (3,400ft)
TIME: 6 hours

ASSESSMENT: Good stalkers' paths give an easy ascent to and descent from a craggy corrie skyline, where a few well-placed iron steps enliven a rugged round with breathtaking views.

SEASONAL NOTES: In winter the ascent to Sgurr Coire nan Eiricheallach remains straightforward, but the ensuing circuit round the skyline of Coire a' Chaorainn, over Sgurr a' Mhaoraich and Am Bathaich, involves the negotiation of steep snow slopes, especially during the crossing of the bealach between the two mountains.

SGURR A' MHAORAICH stands in a commanding position between Loch Hourn and Loch Quoich. From Loch Hourn it appears as a great heap of a mountain, but its true nature as a scalloped peak of soaring ridges is more apparent from Loch Quoich, where excellent stalker's paths ease the approach to its craggy summit.

Begin 800m west of Quoich Bridge, just round the first right-hand bend. A well-graded path weaves to and fro up Bac nan Canaichean on the south ridge of Sgurr Coire nan Eiricheallach. Convex slopes conceal the route ahead but there is an extensive panorama of Loch Quoich mountains behind. Higher up, the

Ben Vane above a sea of cloud, from the north-east ridge of Ben Ime (Route 2/3)

The north-east ridge of Beinn an Lochain (Route 4)

Climbing the north-west ridge of Ben Challum in winter (Route 6)

Beinn a' Chreachain from Beinn Achaladair (Route 7)

A spring day on Creag Mhor: the summit from Sron nan Eun
(Route 8)

An Alpine day on Beinn a' Chochuill: approaching the summit,
with Beinn Eunaich behind left (Route 11)

The impressive north face of Stob a' Ghlais Choire under snow
(Route 16)

Sgurr Dhomhnuill from Druim Garbh (Route 23)

Spring snow on the Druim Chosaidh, looking eastwards from
Sgurr a' Choire-bheithe (Route 30)

Sgurr a' Mhaoraich from Gleouraich to the east (Route 33)

The South Glen Shiel Ridge from the slopes of Sgurr an Fhuarail across the glen (Route 34)

Sgurr Breac and Toman Coinich viewed across Toll an Lochain from Sron na Goibhre (Route 39)

Crazy paving on Arkle's narrow summit ridge (Route 42)

The summit of Sgor Gaoith above Loch Einich (Route 45)

The Devil's Point from the Lairig Ghru in the depths of winter
(Route 46)

Beinn Mheadhoin and the Sticil from the Cairn Gorm plateau
(Route 47)

ridge becomes more well-defined and easy-angled. The map shows the path ending at 670m but long sections of it continue above this point. The going is so easy that the only time the path is really useful is on the steep summit slopes of Sgurr Coire nan Eiricheallach.

The Sgurr stands at the lip of Coire a' Chaorainn and marks the start of the round of the craggy corrie skyline, with the continuing ridge becoming rockier and more interesting as it undulates across a bealach to the complex summit of Sgurr a' Mhaoraich. Approaching the summit, the main path keeps left of rock outcrops on the ridge crest, but the direct route over them gives some very pleasant, very mild scrambling. In a couple of places you will find the rusted remains of some old iron steps and railings, which enables the route to stake a claim as Scotland's one and only *via ferrata*.

The last steep rise to the summit requires further mild handwork, and in mist note that there is a dip about 100m before the large summit cairn. On a good day the view down fjord-like Loch Hourn, past Rum and Skye to the Outer Hebrides, is spectacular.

Continuing round the rim of Coire a' Chaorainn, keep close to the cliff edge for a close-up view of the pinnacle seen on ascent. Soon you reach an ill-defined junction of ridges from where steep slopes of stones and grass descend awkwardly to a bealach. Before you descend, it is worth making the half-hour return trip to Sgurr a' Mhaoraich Beag for an uninterrupted view along Loch Hourn. From the bealach, more steep, rocky slopes rise to the long summit ridge of Am Bathaich, a Top in Munro's Tables until demoted in 1974.

Not far beyond the last rise on the ridge a stalkers' path is picked up. This becomes boggy in places lower down but otherwise gives an untroubled descent to Glen Quoich, where it continues through mixed woodland and past a fine waterfall on the Allt Coire a' Chaorainn to join a Land Rover track back to Quoich Bridge.

ROUTE 34 **THE SOUTH GLEN SHIEL RIDGE**

	1	2	3	4	5
GRADE				X	
TERRAIN	X				
NAVIGATION			X		
SERIOUSNESS			X		

OS MAP: 33
GR: 014040
DISTANCE: 34km (21 miles)
ASCENT: 1,830m (6,000ft)
TIME: 12 hours

ASSESSMENT: A route that rivals the Five Sisters of Kintail as the classic West Highland ridge walk, traversing no less than seven Munros (and with opportunities for more).

SEASONAL NOTES: A spectacular and considerable winter expedition, for fit experts only, best tackled from Glen Shiel using transport at both ends. A good introduction for aspiring winter ridge walkers is the round of Maol Chinn-dearg and Sgurr Coire na Feinne from Glen Shiel by their narrow north-east ridges.

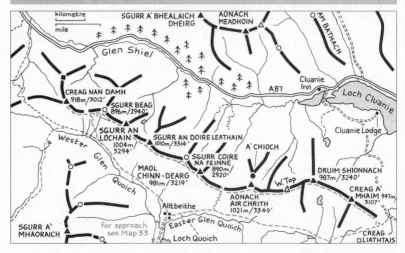

NO RIDGE OUTSIDE the Isle of Skye has so many fine Munros as the South Glen Shiel Ridge. Good stalkers' paths at each end make access easy, but fitness is essential for the complete traverse. If transport can be arranged, a one-way trip is best approached from Glen Shiel to the north, but the best round trip access is from Loch Quoich to the south, using a cart track that runs the whole length of Easter and Wester Glen Quoich.

Beginning at Quoich Bridge, take the Land Rover track to Alltbeithe and turn right in front of the house to follow the cart track up Easter Glen Quoich. Keep going until well beyond the last crags, then branch left at an obvious fork on a path that climbs behind Creag Liathtais to join a wonderfully contoured path up the south-east ridge of Creag a' Mhaim.

The ridge walk proper begins at the summit with the crossing of a shallow saddle to Druim Shionnach; on ascent the ridge narrows to provide the first optional scrambling of the day. A gentle descent and long, undulating re-ascent on grass lead onwards over the West Top (new in 1997) to Aonach air Chrith (see Route 41 in *100 Best Routes*), and then the ridge becomes narrower, rockier and more exposed, with some handwork required, on the steep descent to the next gap.

An equally steep ascent, this time mainly on grass, gains the summit of Maol Chinn-dearg, and then easier slopes descend over the minor top of Sgurr Coire na Feinne (which Munro baggers avoid on a bypass path). Another steep climb (or maybe they just all seem this way by now) gains the summit of Sgurr an Doire Leathain, with more minor scrambling possible on the narrow crest right of the path.

On the next descent the path runs down a very narrow ridge crest, and this is followed by a fitness-testing ascent of conical Sgurr an Lochain, with yet more optional scrambling on the cliff-edge crest. Across the next saddle lies the non-Munro of Sgurr Beag, which all but the pure in heart will bypass on the Munro baggers' traverse path. Then comes the final ascent of the day up Creag nan Damh.

For the easiest way down, return to the last gap and seek out the old stalkers' path, now grassed over, which gives a knee-friendly descent on the left of the main stream to the cart track in Wester Glen Quoich. Before descending, explore a short distance beyond Creag nan Damh to try the best little scramble on the main ridge. You can also continue to the next bealach and descend a stalkers' path from there, and superbaggers should also note the presence of two further Munros (Sgurr na Sgine and the Saddle) much further along.

ROUTE 35 **THE CONBHAIREAN GROUP**

	1	2	3	4	5
GRADE	X				
TERRAIN		X			
NAVIGATION			X		
SERIOUSNESS		X			

OS MAP: 34
GR: 144103
DISTANCE: 16km (10 miles)
ASCENT: 1,260m (4,150ft)
TIME: 7½ hours
ASSESSMENT: Good paths, good terrain and broad, sweeping ridges give easy ridge walking on three Munros and their numerous Tops.
SEASONAL NOTES:
The mountains of the Conbhairean group are the easiest of the Glen Shiel hills in winter. The ascent of Carn Ghluasaid is a good introduction to winter hillwalking. The steeper slopes of Sgurr nan Conbhairean require more care, and the neck of ground leading to Drochaid an Tuill Easaich may also give problems in certain conditions.

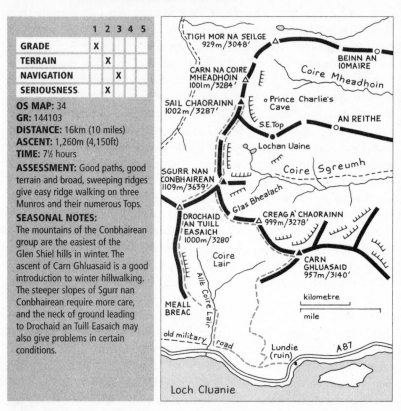

THE GLEN SHIEL hills terminate in the east with a group of three Munros and several Tops that offer grand, open walking on excellent terrain. Their chief feature is a whole series of gaping eastern corries, so wild and remote that Bonnie Prince Charlie was taken there in 1746 to hide from his Redcoat pursuers.

The first Munro, Carn Ghluasaid, is reached by an excellent stalker's path that gives one of the easiest ascents in the Highlands. The path begins at the lay-by on the A87 opposite the ruin of Lundie on the shores of Loch Cluanie. It climbs to follow the line of an old military road, forks right as the main path after about 700m and takes a convoluted but well-graded line up the heathery hillside. It peters out on the short south-west ridge of Carn Ghluasaid and then gentle slopes continue up to the broad summit dome of this first Munro, whose summit cairn lies close to the edge of the first great corrie.

The route onwards goes left round the corrie rim on a wide rolling ridge that gives very pleasant walking on gentle slopes. Creag a' Chaorainn (the first Top) is the next summit reached, and then the rim of the next corrie is followed across the broad, stony saddle of the Glas Bhealach and up steeper slopes to the summit of Sgurr nan Conbhairean, the reigning peak of the group.

A 200m (650ft) descent from Sgurr nan Conbhairean leads on round the next corrie, with two wild lochans nestling far below, and then the ridge narrows to a bealach before broader slopes rise to the summit of Sail Chaorainn, the third Munro.

Two Tops lie further along the ridge. You are recommended to make the short return trip to the first (Carn na Coire Mheadhoin, ½ hour return) along a complex little section of ridge that undulates across a shallow notch round Coire Mheadhoin, whose depths conceal Prince Charlie's Cave. The summit is unmarked but do go to the large cairn just beyond for the view of Loch Affric across the distant second Top (Tigh Mor na Seilge), whose ascent will require a good deal more motivation. Note also that Sail Chaorainn's south-east top was a Top in Munro's Tables until 1981.

To return, re-ascend Sgurr nan Conbhairean as far as the shoulder where the ridge veers left to the summit, then make a rising traverse right on a developing path to gain the south-west ridge. Follow this ridge down across a narrow neck of ground between lochan-filled corries and up to the summit of Drochaid an Tuill Easaich, the last Top of the day. Descend the easy south ridge to Meall Breac, the steep shoulder above Loch Cluanie, and go left down the heathery hillside into Coire Lair to pick up a good path on the far side of the stream. This takes you down to the old military road and back to Lundie.

The
Northern Highlands

ROUTE 36 **THE ROUND OF THE HUNDRED HILLS**

	1	2	3	4	5
GRADE			X		
TERRAIN					X
NAVIGATION					X
SERIOUSNESS					X

OS MAP: 25 (also partly on OL8)
GR: 960569
DISTANCE: 16km (10 miles)
ASCENT: 1,010m (3,300ft)
TIME: 7 hours
ASSESSMENT: A tough, sporting little route for the adventurous, leading through an amazing, maze-like landscape to the summits of two magnificent viewpoints.
SEASONAL NOTES: A challenging winter route. Notable problems include the descent of the canyon-rim of the Allt nan Corrag, ankle-snapping, snow-covered boulder-fields and complex winter terrain where routefinding skills will be tested to the limit, especially in foul weather.
GLACIAL NOTE: A drumlin is a streamlined mound of glacial debris, rounded or elongated in the direction of the original flow of the ice.

THE TWO IGNORED Corbetts on the south side of Glen Torridon unexpectedly offer one of the most adventurous and fascinating rounds in the Highlands. The route begins at the car park opposite Lochan an Iasgair. Walk across the road-bridge and take the well-maintained path round the far side of Lochan an Iasgair, passing the Ling Hut and waterfalls. The path climbs into the Coire of the Hundred Hills, which is named after its countless pimple-like glacial drumlins.

To find the best route up through complex country, keep to the path until it veers right away from the stream that comes down from the lochan at GR 954532, continue up beside the stream to the lochan, then follow the bank of the nearby stream that comes down from the corrie between Sgorr nan Lochan Uaine and Beinn Liath Mhor. A great sweep of slabs just below the corrie gives excellent (optional) friction scrambling, especially on the immediate left of the stream.

The corrie is floored with a chain of superb lochans that would not be out of place in the Rocky Mountains. Walk round the left-hand shorelines of the first two lochans, across fins of sandstone slabs, to reach Lochan Uaine, a larger lochan backed by cliffs. Follow its right-hand shoreline and clamber up easy rocks at the back to reach the watershed, over which lies the fourth, largest and perhaps most magnificent lochan of all. Work your way round its left-hand side until you reach grass slopes that give easy access to the south-east ridge of Sgorr nan Lochan Uaine, where slopes of quartzite rubble climb to a flat mossy summit.

Between here and Sgurr Dubh is the Ridge of the Hundred Hills, a broad ridge dotted with labyrinthine hillocks and lochan-filled rocky hollows that will entertainingly test your route-finding skills to the limit. Attempt to work out a good route before descending onto the ridge. To begin with, quartzite-strewn grass slopes lead down to a saddle, and from here on a guidebook writer can only wish you good luck! Approaching the summit of Sgurr Dubh, the easiest route goes left and tackles the summit slopes from the back.

To descend, first return partway along the ridge. Keep right of the crest, aiming for a string of large lochans, and follow the course of the Allt nan Corrag, the stream that links them. As the stream leaves the ridge, it forms a fantastic canyon with vertical 60m (200ft) walls. With a spot of handwork you can descend the rock-strewn right-hand rim of the canyon to reach an emerging path that continues down through the drumlins beside the stream to rejoin the outward path.

ROUTE 37 **BEINN DEARG (TORRIDON)**

	1	2	3	4	5
GRADE					X
TERRAIN			X		
NAVIGATION					X
SERIOUSNESS					X

OS MAP: 19/24/25 or OL8
GR: 869577
DISTANCE: 18km (11½ miles)
ASCENT: 1,130m (3,700ft)
TIME: 9 hours

ASSESSMENT: A very steep ascent leads to an exhilarating end-to-end scramble along one of the most problematic and exciting ridges in Torridon.

SEASONAL NOTES: Under snow the main ridge provides a major test of winter mountaineering skills. The traverse of The Castle is the crux, but be vigilant also for avalanche-prone slopes buttressing each end of the ridge.

NOTE FOR THE SENSITIVE: The only easy approach to the summit is from remote Coire Mor to the north.

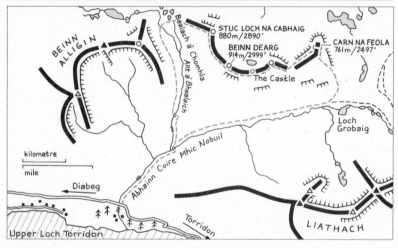

BEINN DEARG is the least climbed of Torridon's major mountains because its metric height of 914m leaves it tantalisingly close to, but short of Munro status. It is nevertheless a worthy prize, with an ascent complicated by intimidatingly steep slopes and a main ridge whose entertaining traverse involves hard scrambling at one point. It is not a mountain for beginners, but for capable scramblers it provides a memorable trip.

Begin as for Beinn Alligin, at the car park at the foot of Coire Mhic Nobuil on the Torridon-Diabeg road, and take the path up the left bank (right side) of the Abhainn Coire Mhic Nobuil. After crossing the river (bridge), keep left at a fork to follow a rougher path up beside the Allt a' Bhealaich and round the foot of Beinn Alligin. When the path approaches the broad, lochan-studded Bealach a' Chomhla, cut right to the foot of Stuc Loch na Cabhaig, Beinn Dearg's northern top.

Forbiddingly steep slopes rise in front of you but they can be tackled direct, at first on very steep grass and then using traces of a path that threads its way up through easy rock bands to a level shoulder. Beyond here the real entertainment starts as the ridge narrows to provide very pleasant easy scrambling on sandstone tors *en route* to the top of Stuc Loch na Cabhaig. Over the top, more handwork follows on a descent to a grassy saddle, and then a path weaves up to the flat summit of Beinn Dearg among sandstone blocks that again give excellent optional scrambling.

The next, complex section of ridge doglegs down over a side buttress to reach The Castle, an imposing rock bastion whose traverse is the most exciting part of the route. As the hardest scrambling cannot be avoided, except by taking to horrendous grass slopes, ignore futile bypass paths and stick to the crest. The ascent is barely a scramble but on descent there are several bands of crags to negotiate. The hardest band, which gives the route its Grade 5 rating, is descended by a 4m (13ft) crack that will give you initial pause for thought (it is best tackled facing inwards). Easier scrambling follows and then you can look back and wonder.

The traverse of the ridge ends on easy slopes of grass and boulders that give you time to admire the hidden northern corries of Liathach. Beyond a minor top and a saddle lies Carn na Feola, the most easterly of Beinn Dearg's tops. After visiting the summit cairn at the far end of a long plateau, return to the near end and descend boulder-strewn slopes towards Loch Grobaig. Bear right at the bottom to rejoin the Coire Mhic Nobuil path.

ROUTE 38 **BEINN AN EOIN**

	1	2	3	4	5
GRADE	X				
TERRAIN		X			
NAVIGATION			X		
SERIOUSNESS		X			

OS MAP: 19 or OL8
GR: 857721
DISTANCE: 21km (13 miles)
ASCENT: 930m (3,050ft)
TIME: 7½ hours
ASSESSMENT: A good path and scenic ridge walk lead to the shapely summit of a freestanding peak hidden deep in the Torridonian heartland.
SEASONAL NOTES: The ascent of Beinn an Eoin's North End and summit slopes may give problems under snow, and the final ridge, though short, can be of Alpine grandeur and difficulty when corniced.
SKINNY DIPPING NOTE: On a hot summer's day, the small but inviting sandy bays at the mouth of Loch na h-Oidhche may prove an irresistible temptation.
CONSERVATION UPDATE NOTE: Following objections by the author and others, a proposed hydroelectric scheme in the area crossed by this route was rejected in 2004. This scheme would have resulted in the construction of access tracks and weirs, including one on Loch na h-Oidhche that would have turned it into a man-made reservoir and eyesore (and destroyed the sandy bays mentioned above).

NORTH OF THE Glen Torridon Munros is a great lochan-strewn east-west divide, and north of this rise three isolated Corbetts, the most attractive of which is Beinn an Eoin. The mountain consists almost entirely of a long, narrowing spine that rises to a sharp summit, which gives aerial views worthy of the mountain's name, meaning Bird Mountain.

The route begins on the A832, at the footbridge opposite the building at the west end of Am Feur-Loch. From here a bouldery path climbs gently between rocky hills to a low bealach from where there is a striking view of the North End of Beinn an Eoin beyond the gorge of the Abhainn a' Gharbh Choire. The improving path threads its way through the gorge and up beside the meanders of the upper river onto the moor. Cross the Abhainn Loch na h-Oidhche on stepping stones (or ford it if it is in spate), taking time out to detour a short distance upstream to view the unusual divergence where it and the Abhainn a' Gharbh Choire divide into two separate rivers.

Beyond the crossing, follow the path up the rise ahead, then climb left up rock-strewn slopes of grass and heather and contour along one of several sandstone terraces to gain the skyline right of Coire Loch na Geala. Once up, note the large cairn that marks the top of the route back down. Steeper slopes rise to the top of the North End and the start of the ridge walk along the mountain's spine, which offers magnificent views westwards over Loch na h-Oidhche to sturdy Baosbheinn and eastwards across Loch Maree to Slioch.

After crossing a broad, grassy saddle to gain Point 715, cross sandstone pavement to a dip, then cross a minor top to reach another dip and the foot of the steep summit pyramid. Climb the pyramid direct to reach a grassy shoulder and a final section of ridge that narrows gracefully to the summit. A path follows the crest, meandering round a couple of small sandstone tors that give optional scrambling.

It is worth continuing a short distance beyond the summit to the top of the craggy southern slopes, from where there is an uninterrupted view across the east-west divide to the tremendous north faces and corries of the Torridon Munros. It is possible for scramblers to find a way down and join the outward path at the head of Loch na h-Oidhche; easier grass slopes among boulders descend to the lochside from the foot of the summit pyramid. On a good day, however, it is best to stay high and retrace your footsteps along the ridge, with an immense northern seascape to lure you homewards.

ROUTE 39 **THE WEST FANNICHS**

	1	2	3	4	5
GRADE			X		
TERRAIN		X			
NAVIGATION				X	
SERIOUSNESS				X	

OS MAP: 19/20
GR: 162761
DISTANCE: 17km (11 miles)
ASCENT: 1,080m (3,550ft)
TIME: 7 hours

ASSESSMENT: A spacious ridge walk with wonderful views of remote mountain country.

SEASONAL NOTES: Considerable cornices overhang the northern corries in winter and fairly steep snow slopes may be encountered, notably on the descents from A' Chailleach to Sron na Goibhre, and from there to Toll an Lochain. For an alternative way down from A' Chailleach, return to Toman Coinich and descend Druim Reidh until a less steep descent can be made into Toll an Lochain.

THE FANNICHS are a group of nine Munros that provide easy, wide-open ridge walking on good terrain. Seven of the Munros form a huge crescent to the north of Loch Fannich and are described in Route 65 in *100 Best Routes*. West of this crescent is a deep bealach that isolates the remaining two Munros into a subgroup that provides a fine hill walk in its own right, on equally exhilarating ridges and with perhaps even better views.

Begin on the A832 7km (4 miles) west of Braemore Junction on the A835 Dingwall-Ullapool road. Take the track that runs beside a small forest plantation to a boathouse on Loch a' Bhraoin, then continue left along an excellent stalkers' path. This climbs high up the left-hand side of the glen of the Allt Breabaig and crosses the bealach that separates the west Fannichs from the rest of the group.

Leave the path at the bealach and climb the curving east ridge of Sgurr Breac, the first Munro. The ridge provides a pleasant ascent on short grass and is narrow enough to give views down each side, with one rocky spot lower down that merits a spot of minor handwork if you keep to the ridge crest. Summit views are extensive and become even better as the round progresses. Beyond the summit lies a subsidiary top, and then the terrain changes temporarily for a steep descent over broken rocks to the bealach below Toman Coinich, a rounded bump that blocks the way to A' Chailleach, the second Munro.

The 70m (230ft) ascent and descent of Toman Coinich can be avoided if you wish by contouring left round the hillside to the bealach on the far side. A complex and interesting ridge climbs from here to the summit of A' Chailleach; note the place where the ridge bends left higher up. The summit is the best viewpoint in the whole of the Fannichs, with unrivalled views eastwards along Loch Fannich and westwards to the mountains of the Great Wilderness.

To descend, return to the bend in the ridge then keep left down steep slopes onto Sron na Goibhre, a pleasant little ridge that provides a level stroll round the rim of Toll an Lochain, a deep corrie adorned by a sizeable lochan. Avoid the crags at the end of the ridge by descending steeply right to the lip of the corrie, then continue down beside the outlet stream. Minor handwork may be necessary at a band of broken crags lower down. Beyond here, cross the stream, round the craggy end of Druim Reidh and cross easy ground high above Loch a' Bhraoin to rejoin the approach path at the end of the loch.

ROUTE 40 **THE GLENSGUAIB CIRCUIT**

	1	2	3	4	5
GRADE	X				
TERRAIN		X			
NAVIGATION				X	
SERIOUSNESS			X		

OS MAP: 20
GR: 182853
DISTANCE: 23km (14 miles)
ASCENT: 1,160m (3,800ft)
TIME: 9 hours

ASSESSMENT: A striking assortment of glens, cliffs, waterfalls and lochans characterise a wonderfully scenic round of two hidden Munros, reached by excellent stalker's paths.

SEASONAL NOTES:
A straightforward route for competent winter hillwalkers, providing the correct line is taken on the descent to the Ceann Garbh-Eididh nan Clach Geala bealach. Gleann na Sguaib receives no sunlight in winter; its awesome cliffs become festooned with fabulous icefalls and the path up it may become a ribbon of ice.

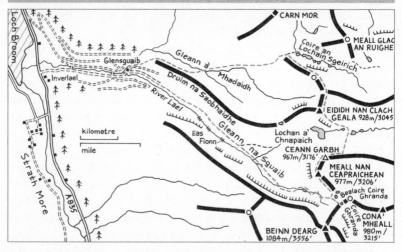

THE SIX MUNROS spread out to the east of the A835 south of Ullapool sport such a wealth of complex mountain scenery that several different approach routes are needed to fully appreciate the area. Routes 69 and 70 in *100 Best Routes* explore the southern and northern boundaries of the group. The route described here crosses the two Munros in the heart of the region, using two excellent stalkers' paths that take you almost all the way up and down the mountains.

Begin at the phone box at Inverlael, near the head of Loch Broom, and take the forest track into the woods beside the River

Lael. Ignoring all side tracks, keep to the main track until it crosses the river, climbs to a fence and forks. Take the right branch to reach the forest boundary and a continuing path up Gleann na Sguaib beside the river. This long, magnificent glen is one of the best mountain approaches in the Highlands. It has waterfalls, lochans, an imposing wall of cliffs 5km (3 miles) long and, at its head, the great U-shaped portal of the Bealach Coire Ghranda, framed between the cliffs of Meall nan Ceapraichean and Beinn Dearg.

Beyond Eas Fionn, the last major waterfall, keep right at a fork to climb along the foot of the wall of cliffs to a beautiful lochan, then follow the path up switchbacks to another pair of lochans on the stony bealach. Before continuing, take a short detour across the bealach to view Coire Ghranda, one of the great corries of the Northern Highlands.

From the bealach a broad, gentle ridge climbs to the summit of Meall nan Ceapraichean, the first Munro, and then stony ground is followed across Ceann Garbh and down to the bealach below Eididh nan Clach Geala, the beautifully named second Munro (see Glossary). Take care not to descend to the bealach until you are directly above it, as a diagonal short-cut involves the negotiation of bands of small crags. The glens on each side of the bealach are decorated with strings of attractive lochans; the largest is Lochan a' Chnapaich at the foot of Eididh nan Clach Geala's craggy south face.

From the bealach a straightforward ascent leads to Eididh nan Clach Geala's summit, marked by the second of two cairns, from where there is a spectacular panorama of Northern Highland peaks. The route then continues northwards across occasionally stony ground to a minor top before descending the broad north-west ridge above Coire an Lochain Sgeirich; keep to the right to see the corrie's string of pearl-like lochans. From the foot of the ridge a good stalkers' path provides a wonderful return route across open moorland and down the crest of Druim na Saobhaidhe to rejoin the approach track.

ROUTE 41 **CUL MOR**

	1 2 3 4 5
GRADE	X
TERRAIN	X
NAVIGATION	X
SERIOUSNESS	X

OS MAP: 15
GR: 127088
DISTANCE: 16km (10 miles)
ASCENT: 1,070m (3,500ft)
TIME: 7 hours

ASSESSMENT: A scenic route past sandy-shored lochs to the triple-topped summit of Coigach's highest mountain.

SEASONAL NOTES: Cul Mor is not normally regarded as a winter mountain, although its ascent from the east or by the ascent route described remains technically easy under snow. The difficult descent route described should be avoided in winter.

NNR UPDATE NOTE: The area through which this route passes was for 41 years a National Nature Reserve, but in 2003 it had to be de-listed owing to the desire of local landowners to keep numbers of sheep and deer high for commercial reasons. It remains protected as a Special Area of Conservation under the European Commission Habitats Directive.

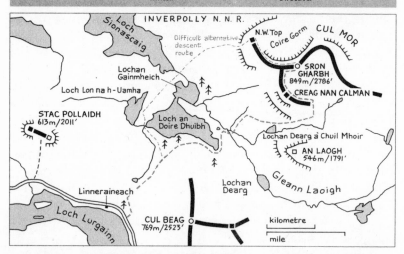

CUL MOR is the highest mountain and best viewpoint in Coigach. It is normally climbed by its dull eastern slopes but its best features lie hidden on the other side, where the 600m (2,000ft) south-west face towers over a secret mountain cirque floored by a collection of beautiful sandy-shored lochs. The picturesque cirque until recently formed the heart of Inverpolly National Nature Reserve (see above), and an ascent of Cul Mor from here is the only approach that does the mountain justice.

The path to Inverpolly NNR begins a few miles along the minor road from Drumrunie junction, near Ledmore on the A835; look for the start of the path a few hundred metres east of Linneraineach, on the east side of a small stand of pine trees. The path climbs over a low bealach between Stac Pollaidh and Cul Beag to reveal the imposing south-west face of Cul Mor ahead. When the path forks, keep right to descend through picturesque woods to the sandy bay at the head of Loch an Doire Dhuibh. The path ends a short distance further along at the river in Gleann Laoigh, which can usually be crossed dryshod just upstream beyond a confluence.

Once across the river, climb boulder-strewn grass slopes onto a broad grassy shelf about one quarter way up the mountain. Follow this shelf right beneath the crags of the south-west face to Lochan Dearg a' Chuil Mhoir, which has a magnificent sandy beach. Follow the rocky glen above the loch to a large grassy basin at the foot of Creag nan Calman's south-east ridge.

Climb the ridge, on heather at first then more easily on grass and finally on flat rocks, to reach the cliff-edge summit. The tremendous view from here is dominated by Stac Pollaidh, soaring above a loch-studded landscape. Continue down to a sandy saddle and then climb lawn-like grass to reach the small pyramid of rock debris that caps Sron Gharbh, Cul Mor's highest point, from where there is an equally tremendous view of Suilven.

Ordinary mortals should return by the route of ascent. There is an alternative descent for the cloven-footed or experienced scrambler, but heed this warning: it is steep and loose and it greatly increases the difficulty and seriousness of the route. Walk out to Cul Mor's north-west top and go straight off the end. Crags force you onto steep rubble in a gully on the left, which it is important to leave a few hundred feet down. Cross to a small grassy saddle on the right-hand ridge and descend an easier (though still awkward) gully on its far side. Once down, ford the river at the southern end of Loch Sionascaig and pick up a path that joins the outward path at the fork mentioned above.

ROUTE 42 **ARKLE**

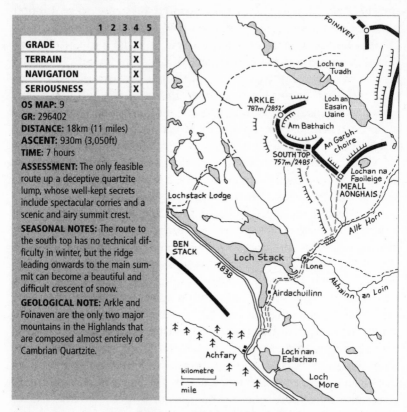

	1	2	3	4	5
GRADE				X	
TERRAIN				X	
NAVIGATION				X	
SERIOUSNESS				X	

OS MAP: 9
GR: 296402
DISTANCE: 18km (11 miles)
ASCENT: 930m (3,050ft)
TIME: 7 hours

ASSESSMENT: The only feasible route up a deceptive quartzite lump, whose well-kept secrets include spectacular corries and a scenic and airy summit crest.

SEASONAL NOTES: The route to the south top has no technical difficulty in winter, but the ridge leading onwards to the main summit can become a beautiful and difficult crescent of snow.

GEOLOGICAL NOTE: Arkle and Foinaven are the only two major mountains in the Highlands that are composed almost entirely of Cambrian Quartzite.

FROM MOST ANGLES Arkle looks like a great lump of a mountain hung with unpromising quartzite cliffs and screes, but appearances are deceptive. Its hidden north side has been gouged out by glaciers to leave a thin ridge slung between two tops, high above a scenic coastline. Owing to the mountain's quartzite skirt there is only one way up, but it is a route of much interest.

Begin at the south end of Loch Stack and take the private road past the house at Airdachuilinn to the private bothy at Lone. When the track bears right just beyond the bridge at Lone, fork left on a less distinct path. This crosses the Allt Horn by a bridge, improves and goes between the Pillars of Horn (two large rocks) to enter a fine wood at the foot of the gorge of the Allt Horn. The path zigzags up the hillside beside the gorge to outflank Arkle's cliffs and enter a steep-sided upper glen.

From here, rough slopes strewn with quartzite rocks rise to Arkle's south top. To find the most pleasant way up, aim diagonally right for the summit of Meall Aonghais. After crossing the stream that comes down from the south top, climb a highway of easy-angled slabs to reach the rock wasteland that is the summit of Meall Aonghais.

On the plateau further right is the beautiful rock-bound Lochan na Faoileige, but the route onwards goes left, crossing a small dip and climbing stony but easy slopes to Arkle's south top. Keep close to the rim of deep An Garbh-choire to pass a great chasm in the cliffs and gain spectacular views of Foinaven's narrow summit ridge across Loch an Easain Uaine (Route 76 in *100 Best Routes*).

From the south top's spacious summit plateau the main summit can be seen ahead atop a thin wall on the far side of the perfect, glacially scoured bowl of Am Bathaich. A path has developed round the bouldery rim. A steep descent is followed by a steep re-ascent to a shoulder, then a short stroll leads to a final section of narrow ridge that guards the summit. The crest is formed by a rib of broken rock that provides the best entertainment on the route. At first it is quite sharp, then it becomes a curious rooftop of deeply fissured crazy paving. Although barely a scramble, its situation gives it an added frisson, with the depths of Am Bathaich below right and a mosaic of lochan-studded moorland below left.

A return by the same route enables you to enjoy the ridge a second time. On descent from the south summit in good weather, detour right and keep close to the cliff edge to prolong the views.

The Cairngorms

ROUTE 43 **GLAS TULAICHEAN**

	1	2	3	4	5
GRADE		X			
TERRAIN	X				
NAVIGATION		X			
SERIOUSNESS		X			

OS MAP: 43
GR: 091712
DISTANCE: 16km (10 miles)
ASCENT: 690m (2,250ft)
TIME: 5½ hours
ASSESSMENT: A circular tramp in surprisingly remote country west of Glen Shee. A vehicular track all the way to the summit makes ascent easy and gives access to the rim of the finest corrie in the region.

SEASONAL NOTES: The track provides an easy winter ascent. Glas Choire Mhor is magnificent when corniced. The descent route described may become icy, with steep snow in a couple of places; if in doubt, descend by the route of ascent.

RAILWAY NOTE: The Glenlochsie light railway line was built to convey Victorian deer shooters up to the now ruined lodge.

A NUMBER OF routes across the high plateaux of the Cairngorms have been described in *100 Best Routes*. This book recommends a further six routes for those who love sky-high tramps in big empty country.

To the south of Braemar are a dozen or so Munros bisected by the road to the Glen Shee ski slopes. Unfortunately, most of these mountains are dull, featureless and scarred by the ironmongery of ski development. Glas Tulaichean is an exception. It lies far from the crowds and its gentle green ridges harbour the area's best feature – the large deep corrie of Glas Choire Mhor.

Glens on either side of the mountain can be linked to make a fine round of the corrie skyline. The ascent has been eased by the building of a vehicular track all the way to the summit. No true hillwalker can view this development as anything other than vandalism, but the track now exists and it would be masochistic not to use it.

Begin at Dalmunzie Hotel, reached by a private road from the Spittal of Glenshee. Cars can normally be parked at the hotel for a small fee (enquire at Reception). Continue along the paved road to Glenlochsie Farm and the Land Rover track up Glen Lochsie. To avoid a double ford of the Glen Lochsie Burn, leave the track at the first ford and double back up the bed of an old railway line to rejoin the track at the ruins of Glenlochsie Lodge. Keep to the track as it climbs the ridge ahead and makes a rising curve all the way to the summit of Glas Tulaichean. The ascent is one of the easiest in the Highlands, but views left into the remote country east of Beinn a' Ghlo give the route a surprising aura of wildness.

When the track bears left near the summit, go right to reach the trig point, which lies close to the edge of craggy Glas Choire Mhor. Continue left round the corrie rim to descend the grassy spur that separates the corrie from its neighbour Glas Choire Bheag, with great views northwards across Loch nan Eun to a frieze of central Cairngorm summits. Continue down a steepening, then bear right to avoid craggy ground and descend grass slopes into Gleann Taitneach. Cross the river (stepping stones or easy ford) to follow a Land Rover track down this fine steep-sided glen.

Further down the glen the track crosses a side stream at a bridge. Immediately beyond here, cross the main river using a bridge at GR 089724 and follow the far bank to rejoin the Glen Lochsie track near Dalmunzie Hotel. **Note:** the bridge marked on some maps at GR 093712 does not exist.

ROUTE 44 **BROAD CAIRN**

	1 2 3 4 5
GRADE	X
TERRAIN	X
NAVIGATION	X
SERIOUSNESS	X

OS MAP: 44
GR: 310851
DISTANCE: 22km (14 miles)
ASCENT: 690m (2,250ft)
TIME: 8 hours

ASSESSMENT: A long, pleasant walk to the summit of an easy Munro, through a landscape that is both picturesque and dramatic.

SEASONAL NOTES: No especial difficulties in winter, but beware cornices on Creag an Dubh Loch and do not underestimate the length of the route under snow.

ROCK NOTE: The crags of Creag an Dubh Loch form the highest continuous rock face in the Cairngorms, reaching a height of 270m (900ft) and sporting many hard rock climbs.

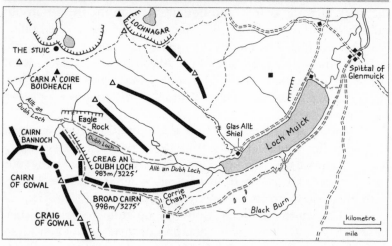

THE BEST FEATURES of the mountains of the White Mounth plateau south of Deeside lie on their northern flanks, and the most interesting ascents are made from this side. Broad Cairn, the most attractive summit on the plateau, is thus best approached from near Ballater via the fine glacial valley of Glen Muick. At the head of the glen is Loch Muick, the largest loch in the whole Cairngorms region, and further up the glen lies Creag an Dubh Loch, one of the highest major crags in Britain. Good tracks and paths make access easy and the complete round adds up to a long but delightfully easy day out.

Begin at the end of the minor road up Glen Muick, which leaves the B976 just outside Ballater. Take the Land Rover track that continues straight on and keep right at a fork a few hundred metres beyond the Spittal of Glenmuick to follow the track along the shores of Loch Muick, which is dramatically situated between steep hillsides.

At the bridge over the Black Burn there are two possible routes onward – the continuing track (known as the Streak of Lightning), which zigzags up to and runs along the edge of the plateau above the loch – or the Diagonal Path, which continues along the lochside and climbs Coire Chash. The choice is yours, but the former gives the best views. The two routes reunite on the saddle at the head of Coire Chash, where Allan's Hut offers some rudimentary shelter.

Beyond the saddle the track becomes much rougher, but a good path continues beside it, becoming indistinct among boulders as it climbs Broad Cairn's summit cone. Other Munros dot the rolling White Mounth plateau, including Lochnagar, but this is more interestingly tackled from elsewhere (see Route 81 in *100 Best Routes*).

To continue the round, descend westwards to a shallow saddle and then bear right, away from the main path (care in mist), to cross the summit of Creag an Dubh Loch. Keeping close to the cliff edge adds a touch of excitement to this part of the route, with vertiginous views down across the Dubh Loch to Eagle Rock and its waterfall. Rough ground continues down to the Allt an Dubh Loch, on whose far side will be found a developing path that descends past fine waterslides to the sandy beaches at the head of the loch – a magnificent spot sandwiched between awesome crags.

From near the mouth of the loch an excellent path descends to Glas Allt Shiel, a private lodge built by Queen Victoria in 1869, and then a Land Rover track continues along the north shore of Loch Muick. At the end of the loch, branch right on a path that crosses to rejoin the outward route.

ROUTE 45 **THE GLEN FESHIE HILLS**

	1	2	3	4	5
GRADE	X				
TERRAIN	X				
NAVIGATION					X
SERIOUSNESS		X			

OS MAP: 36
GR: 860060
DISTANCE: 22km (14 miles)
ASCENT: 1,100m (3,600ft)
TIME: 9 hours
ASSESSMENT: A long, scenic, high-level stravaig, with good approach paths, good terrain and far-ranging views.
SEASONAL NOTES: The route remains technically easy in winter but is of challenging length when the approach paths are obliterated by snow. However, the gentle hillsides of Glen Markie make route curtailment possible at several points. Beware cornices overhanging Loch Einich, and avoid the route in adverse weather owing to difficult routefinding.
PATH UPDATE NOTE: (1) It is now easier to approach Glen Markie by the forest track that begins just south of Lagganlia (GR 858032). (2) With the popularity of Munro baggers' paths further up Glen Feshie, the Glen Markie paths are now little used and have stretches of poor going. Persevere. (3) Instead of descending from Creag Dhubh into Coire Follais, descend the corrie's southern arm to Creag Follais, from whose weather instruments an excellent path zigzags down south-west to the footbridge at GR 881044, to rejoin the track back to Lagganlia.

THE THREE GREAT plateaux of the central Cairngorms are bounded on the west by the trench of Gleann Einich, which is in turn bounded on its west by a mountain wall that rises 600m (2,000ft) to a broad high ridge crowned by Sgor Gaoith. The eastern side of this ridge slopes down more gently to Glen Feshie, where old stalkers' paths in adjacent corries give easy access to a fine round over the high ground.

Begin at Dalnavert, 1½ miles (2km) north of Feshiebridge on the B970, and take the forest track southwards across the Moor of

Feshie. Go straight on at a crossroads, ignore side tracks to right and left, then fork right at a left-hand bend to follow an overgrown track out of the forest to the Allt Coire Follais. Go right along the bank for a few hundred metres, until you can cross easily at the confluence with the Allt a' Mharcaidh, then follow the near bank of the Allt a' Mharcaidh upstream into a beautifully wooded gorge. Cross a footbridge at GR 881044 to reach the start of a forest road (about 40m down the far bank), then branch left at an immediate junction to follow the road to its end at a forest fence. (But see Path Update Note 1)

Go left at the forest fence on a developing path that crosses the Allt nan Cuileach and climbs out onto the open hillside, following a line of intermittent wooden posts. The path improves with height and at 600m bears left round Geal-charn into the upper reaches of Glen Markie, eventually ending at a saddle near the summit of Meall Buidhe.

Now the route develops into a wonderful high-level stravaig on short turf, with glorious views across Speyside. Cross Meall Buidhe and a smaller rise, then bear right to gain the summit of Sgor Gaoith, perched dramatically at the cliff edge above Loch Einich. Look for A' Chailleach (The Old Woman), the pinnacle low down on Pinnacle Ridge (the rock rib to the south).

Continue northwards across a saddle to Sgoran Dubh Mor then descend gently past Sgoran Dubh Beag on a path of pleasant granite granules – superb walking with superb views. Beyond a saddle a short ascent past a number of small granite tors, including Clach Choutsaich and The Argyll Stone, gains Creag Dubh, the last top of the day. From here, go left down easy-angled, heathery slopes into Coire Follais and pick up a path that descends steeply into woods on the right bank of the stream. When open ground is reached again, the path crosses the stream beside a prominent birch tree and descends to join a good Land Rover track that leads back to the Moor of Feshie and the outward route. (But see Path Update Note 3)

ROUTE 46 **THE DEVIL'S POINT**

	1	2	3	4	5
GRADE	X				
TERRAIN	X				
NAVIGATION		X			
SERIOUSNESS					X

OS MAP: 43
GR: 064898
DISTANCE: 32km (20 miles)
ASCENT: 720m (2,350ft)
TIME: 10 hours

ASSESSMENT: Excellent paths lead through the scenic Cairngorm heartland to the summit of a spectacular rock peak.

SEASONAL NOTES: A long winter's day that can be broken at Corrour bothy (rough shelter or camping). The exit from Coire Odhar becomes a steep slope of unbroken snow, often corniced in the depths of winter and with snow patches that last well into spring.

ANATOMICAL NOTE: 'Point' is a prudish Victorian euphemism for 'Penis', which is the correct meaning of the Gaelic 'Bod'.

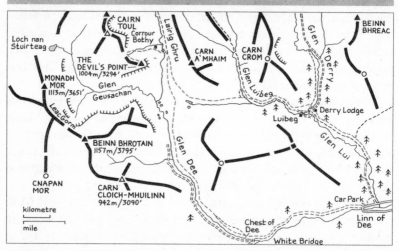

IN THE HEART of the Cairngorms, at the junction of Glen Geusachan and the Lairig Ghru, stands the spectacular portal of rock known as Bod an Deamhain (The Devil's Point). A 13km (8 mile) walk-in hides this most unusual of all Cairngorm Munros from the casual visitor but will not dissuade the true hillwalker, for the approach has great beauty and the summit perch is an incomparable viewpoint that is surprisingly easy to reach.

The route begins at Linn of Dee car park, from the back of which a path joins the Land Rover track along peaceful Glen Lui to Derry Lodge, set among some of the finest Old Scots Pines in the country. Just beyond the lodge, cross the River Lui (footbridge) and branch left on a path that soon becomes a beautiful sandy ribbon through the picturesque pines of Glen Luibeg.

After crossing the Luibeg Burn (on stepping stones or a bridge further upstream), follow the path up and around the shoulder of Carn a' Mhaim to descend into Glen Dee, with the Devil's Point now visible ahead across the River Dee. The mountain's craggy appearance makes it seem impregnable (if that is a term that can be used in connection with *Bod*! – see Anatomical Note), but there is an easy route up round the back from Corrour bothy. The path joins another from White Bridge (see below), and from this junction a side path crosses the River Dee (footbridge) to the bothy.

The climb from here to the summit is a bothy dweller's training exercise of barely 450m (1,480ft). An unmistakable path climbs directly up the hillside into Coire Odhar, a shallow corrie of grass and heather with an attractive waterslide at its back. The path crosses the stream, zigzags up beside the waterslide and traverses back left across the stream near the top to emerge onto the granite plateau above. The final traverse is becoming worn and it is perhaps better to stay beside the stream, especially on the way down. Go left across the plateau and up boulder slopes to reach the summit and a spectacular view of the central Cairngorms.

After descending to the bothy, vary the return route by taking the White Bridge path. Although a bit rougher and a mile longer, this avoids the 60m (200ft) climb back over to Derry Lodge and stays close to the River Dee, which has some beautiful pools and cascades, especially at the Chest of Dee. From White Bridge a Land Rover track continues the last 5km (3 miles) back to the Linn of Dee.

Tigers' Note: Super-fit walkers can easily extend the route beyond the Devil's Point, for example to Cairn Toul (climbed from the other side by Route 82 in *100 Best Routes*). Another long but attractive extension contours round the rim of Glen Geusachan and returns across the vast plateau-mountains of Beinn Bhrotain and Monadh Mor to reach the Land Rover track on the west side of the River Dee.

ROUTE 47 **BEINN MHEADHOIN**

	1	2	3	4	5
GRADE					X
TERRAIN		X			
NAVIGATION					X
SERIOUSNESS					X

OS MAP: 36
GR: 989060
DISTANCE: 18km (11 miles)
ASCENT: 1,480m (4,850ft)
TIME: 9 hours

ASSESSMENT: An adventurous approach through striking country leads to the tor-crowned summit of a superbly situated mountain.
Note: The easiest lines reduce the grade from 5 to 3 or 4.

SEASONAL NOTES: In winter the Fiacaill Ridge is a climber's route, but the ascent of easy-angled Fiacaill a' Choire Chais remains straightforward. Large amounts of snow accumulate at the head of Loch Avon, making the steep lower sections of Coire Domhain and Coire Raibeirt out of bounds to hikers for much of the year. The only easy winter approach to Beinn Mheadhoin is from Glen Derry on the Braemar side.

AS ITS NAME implies, Beinn Mheadhoin (Middle Mountain) occupies an enviable situation in the heart of the Cairngorm mountains, its summit plateau crowned by a *barn* (tor) whose ascent requires a moderate scramble. The shortest route to the peak is an exceptionally interesting one that passes through a spectacular landscape and includes a considerable descent.

Begin at Coire Cas car park at the foot of the Cairn Gorm ski slopes. Take the obvious path round the foot of Fiacaill a' Choire-Chais, then branch left to climb the bouldery lower slopes of the Fiacaill Ridge between Coire an t-Sneachda and Coire an Lochain.

Beyond a subsidiary top a fine ridge of great granite blocks rises to the plateau above. The crest is a hard, exciting scramble but there is easier ground to the right, where a loose path provides an ascent that is barely a scramble at all.

Once onto the plateau, follow the plateau rim down to the bealach at the head of shallow Coire Domhain and descend into the corrie. Lower down, a rough path on the left bank of the stream descends steeply into the wonderfully wild, rock-ringed basin at the head of Loch Avon, a superb spot that rivals Loch Coruisk on Skye for the magnificence of its setting.

Cross the Feith Buidhe as soon as you reach it (this may be difficult when it is in spate) and seek out the historic Shelter Stone, the huge cairned boulder that lies at the foot of the Sticil, one of the finest crags in Britain. From here an obvious path climbs diagonally across the hillside to Loch Etchachan, from where easy slopes of gravel and flat boulders continue up to Beinn Mheadhoin. The broad, almost level summit ridge gives a fine walk that crosses the south-west top and ends at a line of tors that give good optional scrambling.

On the way back down to Loch Avon, detour right across a shallow bealach to the subsidiary Top of Stacan Dubha for the view down to the loch. Recross the Feith Buidhe in the vicinity of the Shelter Stone and walk down to the beautiful sandy bay at the head of the loch. From here a path climbs diagonally across the hillside to join another path on the left bank (right side) of the stream that comes down from Coire Raibeirt.

The Coire Raibeirt path is very steep and eroded at first, which makes for a sporting ascent that requires some handwork. By following the stream all the way to the back of the shallow upper corrie you will reach the top of Fiacaill a' Choire-Chais (difficult to locate in mist; look for a cairn on a large boulder); a path descends from here to the car park.

ROUTE 48 **BEINN A' BHUIRD**

	1	2	3	4	5
GRADE		X			
TERRAIN	X				
NAVIGATION					X
SERIOUSNESS					X

OS MAP: 43/36
GR: 187914
DISTANCE: 35km (21½ miles)
ASCENT: 1,080m (3,550ft)
TIME: 12 hours
ASSESSMENT: A long day in wild country on excellent paths and terrain, exploring a vast plateau edged by great corries.

SEASONAL NOTES: In winter Beinn a' Bhuird's eastern corries carry stupendous cornices and the summit plateau has an Arctic ambience. Care is required on the steep descent to the Sneck. To make the summit easier to reach on a short winter's day, you can camp overnight in the Slugain where the track crosses the burn.

PATH UPDATE NOTE: (1) The path north of the Slugain has been greatly improved and is now a joy to walk. It is still being extended up towards Clach a' Chleirich. The left branch to Carn Fiaclach has seen better days and is in a poor state. Stick with it; it improves once it leaves the moor behind. (2) The steep gravelly descent from Cnap a' Chleirich to the Sneck is so worn that it is almost an unstable scree run in places. Stay well clear of the cliff edge to find a zigzagging path that is the easiest way down.

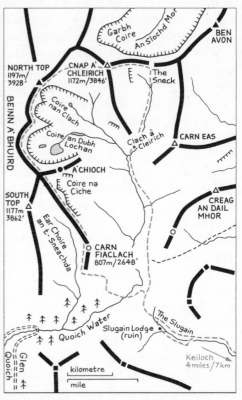

THE GREAT ROLLING tableland of the eastern Cairngorms contains Britain's tenth (Beinn a' Bhuird) and sixteenth (Ben Avon) highest mountains, connected by a narrow neck of ground known as the Sneck. Route 85 in *100 Best Routes* explores Ben Avon from the north; this route tackles Beinn a' Bhuird from the south. The mountain's 3km (2 mile) long summit plateau is bordered on the east by a series of great corries whose rim walk offers some of the most majestic and far-ranging views in the country.

As befits a mountain of its stature, Beinn a' Bhuird is not reached without effort. The 10km (6 mile) walk-in to its foot begins at Keiloch, just off the A93 5km (3 miles) east of Braemar.

From here take the Land Rover track up Gleann an t-Slugain. New track building may outdate your map and these route directions; at the time of writing, follow a signposted route round Alltdourie Farm, then keep left at the first fork and right at the second.

You emerge from woods to enter the open upper glen and the rocky narrows of the Slugain (Gullet), where the poignant ruins of Slugain Lodge stand. The track becomes barely more than a path and forks to provide routes through the Slugain on either side; take one on the way out and the other on the way back – both are interesting.

Above the Slugain the path crosses a low bealach and enters the upper reaches of Glen Quoich at the foot of Beinn a' Bhuird. Keep left at a fork and follow the path down to and across the Quoich Water (which may require a ford). The path continues up the right side of Ear Choire an t-Sneachda and deposits you on the saddle behind Carn Fiaclach. From here you can clamber up a steep boulder slope, or outflank the boulders in a grassy corrie on the left, to reach Beinn a' Bhuird's summit plateau. A detour further left is required to gain the featureless South Top, but more interesting is a detour right to scramble up A' Chioch (The Breast), the rock 'castle' that separates Coire na Ciche from Coire an Dubh Lochan.

The plateau walk continues round the rims of Coire an Dubh Lochan and Coire nan Clach to the summit (north top). It is a wonderfully spacious walk with limitless views, although a nightmare to navigate in cloud. From the summit, continue across a dip to the tor on the highest point of Cnap a' Chleirich (GR 108010), then descend steeply to the Sneck. Pause to view the immense open spaces of An Slochd Mor (The Great Pit) to the north, then head southwards down the right hand side of the burn to pick up an improving path. This passes the prominent boulder called Clach a' Chleirich and eventually rejoins the outward path.

'A delightful expedition.'
Queen Victoria's verdict on the route in 1850

The Islands

ROUTE 49 **ULLAVAL AND OREVAL**

	1	2	3	4	5
GRADE			X		
TERRAIN		X			
NAVIGATION				X	
SERIOUSNESS		X			

OS MAP: 13
GR: 053078
DISTANCE: 15km (9½ miles)
ASCENT: 910m (3,000ft)
TIME: 6 hours

ASSESSMENT: A scenic ridge walk across four tops, on good terrain that allows plenty of time to savour the superb Outer Hebridean views. A visit to the largest overhang in the British Isles is an optional extra.

SEASONAL NOTES: In winter the ascent of Ullaval and the traverse to Oreval remain easy. The only difficulties likely to be encountered are on the steep descent from Oreval and the ascent of Cleiseval's rock band but, with care, these sections should not cause undue problems for experienced and suitably equipped winter walkers.

PERSEVERANCE NOTE: The first ascent of the Great Overhang of Sron Ulladale took six days in 1969.

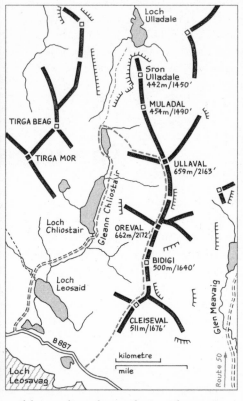

SEEKERS AFTER SOLITUDE could spend weeks exploring the remote, rugged, shapely peaks of North Harris and West Lewis. Route 100 in *100 Best Routes* describes an ascent of Clisham, the highest peak, while this book recommends two more fascinating routes. Ullaval and Oreval are the two highest points on the ridge that runs north-south between the deep glens of Gleann Chliostair and Glen Meavaig. The overhang of Sron Ulladale at the north end of this ridge is one of the natural wonders of Britain.

The route begins at the foot of Gleann Chliostair on the B887 and passes four lochs on its way up the rugged glen. A paved road gives swift access to the dam at Loch Chliostair and then a superb path continues along the lochside, climbs to the higher Loch Ashavat and contours round its western shore to the watershed. The route leaves the path here to make an ascent of Ullaval but, unless you are pressed for time, you should first descend the path on the far side of the watershed to Loch Ulladale, to view the spectacular, overwhelming rock prow of Sron Ulladale (add on 4km/2½ miles, 180m/600ft, 1¼+ hours).

From the watershed, make directly for the summit of Ullaval, which can be seen ahead. Climb grassy slopes among boulders to reach an open bowl that shelves gently up to the summit boulder-cap. The summit cairn stands at the lip of a steep drop into Glen Meavaig, across which rise the twin tops of Teilesval and Uisgnaval Mor (Route 50), backed by Clisham. The route to Oreval continues down a narrow grassy ridge, passing a rock castle that yields to a pleasant scramble or which can easily be bypassed. From the bealach between the two mountains, broader slopes sweep up to the summit of Oreval (take care in mist not to veer left onto a spur ridge).

From Oreval there is a wonderful view of the remainder of the ridge as it snakes over the two lower tops of Bidigi and Cleiseval, with the fantastic sandy beaches of South Harris glistening beyond. The route descends steeply among boulders before making the short climb over the grassy hump of Bidigi. On the ascent of Cleiseval, a rock band is breached by a path that gives minimal handwork, although more sporting scrambling is possible on either side. Above here, slopes of short turf rise to the last summit of the day.

The broken south-west slopes of Cleiseval make a straight-forward descent route to the road difficult to find from above. The best line to take aims in the general direction of the Soay Sound, but just before the road a band of broken crags, requiring handwork and care, provides a final sting in the tail.

ROUTE 50 **TEILESVAL AND UISGNAVAL MOR**

	1	2	3	4	5
GRADE			X		
TERRAIN				X	
NAVIGATION				X	
SERIOUSNESS			X		

OS MAP: 13
GR: 101063
DISTANCE: 18km (11 miles)
ASCENT: 940m (3,100ft)
TIME: 7 hours

ASSESSMENT: A similar route to Route 49 – an exhilarating end-to-end ridge walk across two steep, conical peaks in typically rugged, scenic North Harris country.

SEASONAL NOTES: The north ridge of Teilesval and the south ridge of Uisgnaval Mor offer straightforward winter ascent routes, but the negotiation of the steep snow slopes on either side of the deep notch that separates the two peaks may prove more daunting.

FURTHER EXPLORATION NOTE: To the west of Clisham and routes 49 and 50 stands conical Tirga Mor, Harris's other 600m (2,000ft) peak.

THE SHAPELY TWIN peaks of Teilesval and Uisgnaval Mor form an attractive grouping from many North Harris viewpoints. Like their neighbours Ullaval and Oreval across Glen Meavaig to the west, they are the high points on an isolated north-south ridge and the logistics of their traverse is uncannily similar to Route 49.

Begin at the foot of Glen Meavaig on the B887 and take the Land Rover track along the glen. The rugged, open glen narrows to a rocky portal where wild Loch Scourst lies between the crags of Caadale Granda and Sron Scourst, an impressive conical crag that looks like a miniature Buachaille Etive Mor. The track continues across an almost imperceptible watershed to end at Loch Voshimid at the north end of the ridge beneath the craggy nose of Sron Ard, yet another of North Harris' many amazing north-facing precipices.

At the fishermen's hut just before the loch, fork right on a good stalkers' path that traverses round the foot of Sron Ard into Glen Stuladale and doubles back to climb the left-hand side of the glen. After an ascent of about 80m (260ft), fork right on a less distinct path that traverses to the River Stuladale. When the path bears away from the river again to continue up to Loch Stuladale, leave it and climb directly up steep grass slopes to gain the skyline on the right. Once on the ridge, broad grass slopes continue upward to Craig Stulaval, passing a rock band that gives excellent (optional) scrambling.

Beyond Craig Stulaval the ridge crosses a shallow saddle before narrowing to provide a beautiful, scenic walk up the summit slopes of Teilesval, with the vast landscapes of West Lewis spread out behind you to the north. The short but attractive summit ridge begins as a level walk on grass and ends on Teilesval's guarding summit crags, where handwork is required among the rocks and boulders.

From the summit, you will probably find more elementary handwork necessary on the steep broken slopes (very confusing in mist) that lead down to the deep notch below Uisgnaval Mor. Similar steep slopes, which become easier with height, then climb straight back up to the summit of this highest peak of the group for a glorious view over the lochs and hills of South Harris. With the hard work of the day now over, the remainder of the route develops into an easy descent of Uisgnaval Mor's grassy south ridge, with that sweeping South Harris panorama before you all the way to lure you homeward. To avoid an irksome moorland crossing, it is best to keep to the ridge until beyond Braigh an Fhais, then make a direct descent right of a small stream to reach your starting point.

Glossary/Index

Note: entries are indexed by route number, not page.

A' Chailleach (A *Chyle*-yach,
The Old Woman) 39
(Fannichs), 45 (Glen Feshie)

A' Chioch (A *Chee*-och,
The Breast) 48

A' Chrois (A Chrosh, The
Cross) 3

Abhainn a' Gharbh Choire (Avin
a *Gharra*v Chorra, River of
the Rough Corrie) 38

Abhainn Chosaidh (Avin Chosey,
River of Nooks) 30, 31

Allt a' Chaol Ghlinne (Owlt a
Chœl *Ghlinn*-ya, Stream of
the Narrow Glen) 6

Allt a' Chinn Bhric (Owlt a
Cheen Vreechk, Stream of
the Trout Head) 28

Allt a' Choire Reidh (Owlt a
Chorra Ray, Stream of the
Level Corrie) 25

Allt a' Chuil Choirean (Owlt a
Choo-il Chorran, Stream of
the Back Corrie) 17

Allt a' Mharcaidh (Owlt a Varkie,
Stream of the Horse) 45

Allt Bealach na h-Innsig (Owlt
*Byala*ch na *Heen*shik,
Stream of the Pass of the
Little Island) 14

Allt Breabaig (Owlt Brepak,
Stream of the Little Kick
(i.e. cleft)) 39

Allt Coire na Cruaiche (Owlt
Corra na *Croo*-iche, Stream
of the Corrie of Mounds) 31

Allt Coiregrogain, see
Coiregrogain 3

Allt Eigheach (Owlt *Aigh*ach,
Shouting (i.e. Noisy) Stream)
19

Allt Glas-Dhoire (Owlt Glass
Durra, Stream of the Green
Grove) 29

Allt Luib Ruairidh (Owlt *Loo*-ib
Roo-*airy*, Stream of Rory's
Bay) 18

Allt Mhoille (Owlt *Vull*-ya,
Slow Stream) 11

Allt na h-Uamha (Owlt na *Hoo*-
aha, Stream of the Cave) 21

Allt na Muidhe (Owlt na *Moo*-
ya, Stream of the Churn) 15

Allt na-Cruaiche (Owlt na *Croo*-
iche, Stream of the
Haystacks or Peatstacks) 24

Allt nan Cailleach (Owlt nan
Kyle-yach, Stream of the Old
Woman) 22

Allt nan Corrag (Owlt nan
Corrak, Stream of the
Forefinger or Left-hand Stilt
of a Plough) 36

Allt nan Cuileac (should be
Cuileag) (Owlt nan Koolak,
Stream of the Fly) 45

Allt nan Meirleach (should be
Mèirleach) (Owlt nan *Mayr*-
lyach, The Stream of the
Robber) 12

Am Bathaich (Am *Bah*-ich,
The Byre) 33 (Sgurr a'

Mhaoraich), 42 (Arkle)

Am Feur-Loch (Am Ferr Loch, The Grass Loch) 38

An Eag (An Aik, The Notch) 27

An Garbh-choire (An *Garrav*-chorra, The Rough Corrie) 42

An Sgor (An Skorr, The Peak) 10

An Slochd Mor (An Slochk Moar, The Big Pit) 48

Aonach air Chrith (*Œn*ach air Chri, Trembling Ridge) 34

Aonach Dubh a' Ghlinne (*Œn*ach Doo a *Ghlinn*-ya, Black Ridge of the Glen) 15

Arkle (Level-topped Mountain) 42

Bac nam Foid (Bachk nam Foaj, Peat Bank) 32

Bac nan Canaichean (Bachk nan *Can*ichan, Bank of the Moss-cotton or Sturgeon) 33

Baosbheinn (*Bœsh*ven, Witch Mountain) 38

Bealach a' Bharnish (*Byal*ach a Varnish, Pass of the Gap) 21

Bealach a' Chomhla (*Byal*ach a *Coal*a, Pass of the Door) 37

Bealach a' Mhaim (*Byal*ach a Vaa-im, Pass of the Moor) 3

Bealach an Easain Duibh (*Byal*ach an Aissan *Doo*-y, Pass of the Black Waterfall) 4

Bealach Coire Ghranda (*Byal*ach Corra Ghranda, Pass of the Ugly Corrie) 40

Bealach Ghlas Leathaid (*Byal*ach

Glass *Lyeh*-at, Green Slope Pass) 6

Bealach Leamhain (*Byal*ach *Leh*-an, Elm Pass) 20

Bealach nan Carn (*Byal*ach nan Carn, Pass of the Cairns) 22

Beinn a' Bhuird (Ben a Voorsht, Table Mountain) 48

Beinn a' Chaorainn (Ben a *Chœr*in, Rowan Mountain) 21

Beinn a' Chlachair (Ben a *Chlach*ar, Mountain of the Mason) 20

Beinn a' Chochuill (Ben a *Choe*-chil, Mountain of the Hood or Shell) 11

Beinn a' Chreachain (Ben a Chrechan, Clam Mountain) 7

Beinn Achaladair (Ben Achallader, poss. Mountain of the Field of Hard Water) 7

Beinn an Eoin (Ben an *Yai*-awn, Bird Mountain) 38

Beinn an Lochain (Ben an Lochin, Mountain of the Lochan) 4

Beinn Chaorach (Ben *Chœr*ach, Sheep Mountain) 6

Beinn Dearg (Ben *Jerr*ak, Red Mountain) 37 (Torridon), 40 (Glensguaib)

Beinn Dubh (Ben Doo, Black Mountain) 2

Beinn Dubhchraig (Ben *Doo*-chraik, Black Crag Mountain) 5

Beinn Eunaich (Ben *Ayn*ich, Fowling Mountain) 11

Beinn Fhionnlaidh (Ben *Hee*-only, Finlay's Mountain) 14

Beinn Ime (Ben *Eem*a, Butter Mountain) 3

Beinn Mheadhoin (Ben *Vai*-an, Middle Hill) 47

Beinn Narnain (obscure) 3

Beinn Resipol (obscure (*pol* is Old Norse for homestead)) 22

Beinn Sgulaird (Ben Skoolarj, poss from Gaelic *sgul* (shelter) + *aird* (height) or *sgulair* (large old hat)) 13

Ben Aden (from Gaelic *Beinn Aodainn*, Face Mountain) 31

Ben Challum (Calum's Mountain) 6

Ben Oss (Deer Mountain or Elk Mountain) 5

Ben Vane (Middle Mountain (from Gaelic *mheadhoin*)) 2

Ben Vorlich (poss. Mountain of the Bay) 1

Bidigi (obscure) 49

Binnein Shuas (*Been*-yan *Hoo*-as, Upper Peak (as opposed to neighbouring Binnein Shios, Lower Peak)) 20

Broad Cairn 44

Cam Bhealach (Cam *Vyal*ach, Crooked Pass) 29

Cam Chreag (Cam Chraik, Crooked Crag) 6

Cam Ghleann (Cam Ghlenn, Crooked Glen) 16

Carn Ban Mor (Big Fair Hill) 45

Carn Dearg (Carn *Jerra*k, Red Cairn) 19

Carn Fiaclach (Carn *Fee*-aclach, Toothed Cairn) 48

Carn Ghluasaid (Carn *Ghloo*asat, Cairn of Movement) 35

Carn Gorm (Carn *Gorra*m, Blue Cairn) 10

Carn Mairg (Carn *Merra*k, Cairn of Pity or Regret) 10

Carn na Coire Mheadhoin (Carn na Corra *Vai*-an, Cairn of the Middle Corrie) 35

Carn na Feola (Carn na Fyolla, Flesh Cairn) 37

Ceann Garbh (Kee-oun *Garra*v, Rough Head) 40

Chno Dearg (Cro *Jerra*k, Red Nut (but more likely a misprint for Cnoc Dearg, Crochk *Jerra*k, Red Hill)) 18

Clach a' Chleirich (Clach a Chleerich, The Cleric's Stone) 48

Clach Choutsaich (Coutts' Stone) 45

Clach Leathad (Clach *Lyeh*-at (usually pronounced *Clach*let), Stone of the Slope) 16

Cleiseval (poss from Norse *klif* (rocky place) and *val* (peak)) 49

Cnap a' Chleirich (Crap a Chlairich, The Cleric's Knoll) 48

Coille Coire Chuilc (*Cull*-ya

Corra *Cool*-ak, Wood of the Reedy Corrie) 5

Coire a' Chaorainn (Corra *Chœr*in, Rowan Corrie) 33

Coire Achaladair, see Beinn Achaladair 7

Coire an Dubh Lochan (Corran Doo Lochan, Corrie of the Black Lochan) 48

Coire an Lochain (Corran Lochin, Corrie of the Lochan) 18 (Treig), 47 (Beinn Mheadhoin)

Coire an Lochain Sgeirich (Corran Lochin *Skair*ich, Corrie of the Skerried Lochan) 40

Coire an t-Sneachda (Corran tchnechda, Snowy Corrie) 47

Coire Ba (Cow Corrie) 16

Coire Ban (Corra Bahn, White Corrie) 9

Coire Buidhe (Corra *Boo*-ya, Yellow Corrie) 5 (Ben Oss), 21 (Beinn a' Chaorainn)

Coire Cas (Corra Cash, Steep Corrie) 47

Coire Chash (Corra Chash, Steep Corrie) 44

Coire Clachaig (Corra *Clach*ak, Stony Corrie) 21

Coire Claurigh (Corra Clowry, obscure) 17

Coire Creagach (Corra *Craik*ach, Craggy Corrie) 1

Coire Daingean (Corra *Din*gan, Firm Corrie) 7

Coire Domhain (Corra *Daw*in, Deep Corrie) 47

Coire Dubh (Corra Doo, Black Corrie) 15

Coire Eigheach, see Allt Eigheach 19

Coire Follais (Corra *Foll*ash, Public Corrie) 45

Coire Garbh (Corra *Garra*v, Rough Corrie) 5

Coire Ghranda (Corra Ghranda, Ugly Corrie) 40

Coire Glas (Corra Glass, Green Corrie) 12

Coire Lair (Corra Lahr, Low Corrie) 35

Coire Leacachain (Corra *Lyechka*chin, Slabby Corrie) 29

Coire Liath (Corra *Lee*-a, Grey Corrie) 32

Coire Loch na Geala (Corra Loch na Gyalla, poss. Corrie of the Leech) 38

Coire Lochain (Corra Lochin, Corrie of the Lochan) 29

Coire Mhic Nobuil (Corra Veechk *Noa*bil, MacNoble's Corrie) 37

Coire Mor Chlachair (Corra Moar *Chlach*ar, Big Corrie of the Mason) 20

Coire na Bantighearna (Corra na Ben-*tyur*-na, The Lady's Corrie) 1

Coire na Ciche (Corra na *Keech*a, Corrie of the Breast) 48

Coire na h-Uamha (Corra na Hoo-aha, Corrie of the Cave) 21

Coire nan Clach (Corra nan Clach, Corrie of the Stones) 48

Coire nan Gall (Corra nan Gowl, Corrie of the Stranger) 31

Coire Odhar Mor (Beag) (Corr Oa-ar Moar (Beck), Big (Little) Dun-coloured Corrie) 29

Coire Odhar (Corr Oa-ar, Dun-coloured Corrie) 46

Coire Pollach (Holey Corrie) 16

Coire Raibeirt (Corra Rabert, Robert's Corrie) 47

Coire Screamhach (Corra Screvach, Disgusting or Ugly Corrie) 25

Coire Sgreumh (poss. should be sgreamh (disgust)) 35

Coire Thollaidh (Corra Hully, Corrie of the Hollow) 32

Coire-cheathaich (Corra Cheh-ich, Corrie of Mist) 8

Coirechoille (Corra Chull-ya, Corrie of the Wood) 17

Coiregrogain (poss. Corrie of the Wrinkled Heather) 2

Corr na Beinne (Corra na Ben-ya, Corrie of the Mountain) 15

Corrour Station (from Gaelic Coire Odhar, Dun-coloured Corrie) 18

Craig Stulaval (Craik Stoolaval, Crag of the Mountain of the Shieling (from Norse stol (shieling) and val (peak))) 50

Crannach Wood (from Gaelic crann (tree) and achadh (field), or crannach (full of trees)) 7

Creag a' Chaorainn (Craik a Chœrin, Rowan Crag) 35

Creag an Dubh Loch (Craik an Doo Loch, Crag of the Black Loch) 44

Creag an Fheadain (Craik an Aiten, Waterpipe Crag) 9

Creag Dhubh (Craik Ghoo, Black Crag) 16

Creag Dubh (Craik Doo, Black Crag) 45

Creag Liathtais (Craik Lee-a-tash, from Gaelic liath (grey) and tais (damp)) 34

Creag Loisgte (Craik lossctye, Burnt Crag) 6

Creag Mhaim (Craik Vaa-im, Breast (-shaped) Crag) 34

Creag Mhor (Craik Voar, Big Crag) 8

Creag nan Calman (Dove Crag) 41

Creag nan Damh (Craik nan Daff, Stag Crag) 34

Creag Pitridh (obscure, poss. from Gaelic pit (farm) and ridhe (field)) 20

Creise (Craish, obscure, poss. from the Gaelic creis (grease)) 16

Cul Mor (Cool Moar, Big Back) 41

Dearg Allt (Jerrak Owlt, Red Stream) 28

Devil's Point, The 46

Drochaid an Tuill Easaich (*Droch*itch an Too-il *Aiss*ach, Bridge of the Hole with Many Waterfalls) 35

Druim a' Chuirn (Drum a Choorn, Ridge of Cairns) 27

Druim Chosaidh (Drum Chosey, Ridge of Nooks) 30

Druim Coire nan Laogh (Drum Corra nan *Lai*-ogh, Ridge of the Corrie of Calves) 26

Druim Garbh (Drum *Garr*av, Rough Ridge) 23

Druim Leac a' Sgiathain (Drum Lyechk a *Skee*-a-han, Ridge of the Winged Slab) 23

Druim na Geid Salaich (poss. should be *Gead*) (Drum na Gyate Sallich, Ridge of the Dirty Spot or Dirty Ridge) 32

Druim na Saobhaidhe (Drum na Sœvy, Ridge of the Fox Lair) 40

Druim Reidh (Drum Ray, Level Ridge) 39

Druim Shionnach (Drum Shoonach, Pipe-reed Ridge) 34

Dubh Loch (Doo Loch, Black Loch) 44

Ear Choire an t-Sneachda (Err Corran *Trech*ka, East Snowy Corrie) 48

Eas Fionn (Aiss Fyoon, Fair Waterfall) 40

Eididh nan Clach Geala (Aijy nan Clach Gyalla, Web of the White Stones) 40

Fannichs, The (poss. The Gentle Slopes) 39

Feith Buidhe (Fay *Boo*-y, Yellow Bog-stream) 47

Fiacaill a' Choire-Chais (*Fee*-achkill a Chorra Chash, Tooth of the Steep Corrie) 47

Fiacaill Ridge, The 47

Fraoch Bheinn (Frœch Ven, Heather Mountain) 28

Gairich (Peak of Roaring or Yelling) 32

Garbh Coire (*Garr*av Corra, Rough Corrie) 48

Garbh-bheinn (*Garr*a-ven, Rough Mountain) 18

Geal Charn (Gyal Charn, White Cairn) 20

Geal-charn (Gyal Charn, White Cairn) 45

Glas Bhealach (Glass *Vyal*ach, Green Pass) 35

Glas Bheinn Mhor (Glass Ven Voar, Big Green Mountain) 12

Glas Choire Mhor (Bheag) (Glass Chorra Voar (Bhake), Big (Little) Green Corrie) 43

Glas Tulaichean (Glass Toolichan, Green Hill) 43

Gleann a' Chlachain (Glen a *Chlach*in, Glen of the Village) 6

Gleann a' Mhadaidh (Glen a Vahty, Glen of the Foxes) 40

Gleann an Lochain Eanaiche
(Glen an Lochin *Yenni*cha,
Glen of the Dandruff
Lochan or Wool Lochan) 26

Gleann an t-Slugain (Glen an
Tlookan, Glen of the Gullet)
48

Gleann Chliostair (Glen Clishter,
Clyster (i.e. Enema) Glen) 49

Gleann Fionnlighe (Glen Fyoon-
lee-ya, Glen of Fingal's Grave)
25

Gleann Laoigh (Glen *Lœ*-y, Calf
Glen) 41

Gleann leac na muidhe (Glen
Lechk na *Moo*-y, Glen of the
Slab of the Horse's Mane)
15

Gleann na Sguaib (Glen na
Skoo-ab, Glen of the Sheaf
of Corn) 40

Gleann Taitneach (Glen Tatnyach,
Delightful Glen) 43

Glen Ceitlein (Glen Caitlin) 12

Glen Dessarry 27, 28

Glen Feshie (from Gaelic
feithsidh (boggy haugh)) 45

Glen Geusachan (Glen
*Gyoos*achan, Glen of the Fir
Trees) 46

Glen Kingie 28

Glen Lyon 10

Glen Markie (Glen of the Horse)
45

Glen Meavaig 50

Glen Shiel 34

Glen Stuladale (Glen of the
Shieling) 50

Glen Torridon 36

Glensguaib, see Gleann na
Sguaib 40

Gulvain, originally Gaor Bheinn
(poss. Filthy Mountain
(from Gaelic *gaorr*) or Noisy
Mountain (from Gaelic
gaoir)) 25

Hundred Hills, The 36

Lairig Ghru (*Lahr*ik Ghroo,
poss. Oozing Pass (from
Gaelic *drudadh*, after the
River Druie) or Gloomy Pass
(from Gaelic *grumach*)) 46

Lairig Leacach (*Lahr*ik
*Lyech*kach, Slabby Pass) 17

Loch a' Bhealaich Leamhain
(Loch a Vyalach *Leh*-an,
Loch of Elm Pass) 20

Loch a' Bhraoin (Loch a *Vrœ*-in,
Showery Loch) 39

Loch an Daimh (Lochan Deff,
Stag Loch) 9

Loch an Doire Dhuibh (Loch an
Jurra *Ghoo*-y, Loch of the
Black Grove) 41

Loch an Easain Uaine (Lochan
Aissan Oo-*an*-ya, Loch of
the Green Waterfall) 42

Loch Avon (Loch Ahn, Fair
Loch) 47

Loch Einich, named after Gleann
Einich (Ennich, Marshy) 45

Loch Grobaig (Loch Grobbak,
Broken-tooth Loch) 37

Loch na h-Oidhche (Loch na
*Hoych*a, Loch of the Night)
38

Loch nan Eun (Loch nan *Yai*-awn, Bird Loch) 43

Loch Quoich (Cuckoo Loch (from Gaelic *cuaich*)) 30, 31, 32, 33

Loch Treig (Loch Traik, Forsaken Loch) 18

Lochan a' Chnapaich (Lochan a *Chrap*ich, Knobbly Lochan) 40

Lochan an Fhigheadair (Lochan an *Fee*-adar, The Weaver's Lochan) 32

Lochan an Iasgair (Lochan an Yaskar, The Fisherman's Lochan) 36

Lochan Dearg a' Chuil Mhoir (Lochan *Jerrak* a *Choo*-il *Voa*-ir, Red Lochan of the Big Back (i.e. a lochan on the slopes of Cul Mor named after the colour of its sandy shore)) 41

Lochan na Faoileige (Lochan na *Fœli*ka, Seagull Lochan) 42

Lochan na h-Earba (Lochan na Hyerba, Roe Lochan) 20

Lochan nam Breac (Lochan nam Brechk, Trout Lochan) 31

Lochan nan Cat (Cat Lochan) 9

Lochan Uaine (Lochan Oo-*an*-ya, Green Lochan) 35 (Conbhairean), 36 (Hundred Hills)

Mam Ban, White Moor 19

Mam na Cloich-Airde (Mam na *Clo*-ich Arja, Moor of the Stoney Height) 26

Maol Chinn-dearg (Mœl Cheen *Jerra*k, Bare Red-headed Hill) 34

Meall a' Bharr (Myowl a Var, Hill of the Crop) 10

Meall a' Bhuiridh (Myowl a Voory, Hill of Rutting) 16

Meall a' Choire Chruinn (Myowl a Chorra *Chroo*-in, Hill of the Round Corrie) 24

Meall a' Choire Dhuibh (Myowl a Chorra *Ghoo*-y, Hill of the Black Corrie) 31

Meall an Spardain (Myowl an Spartan, Hill of the Roost) 30

Meall an t-Slugain (Myowl an Slookan, Hill of the Gullet) 22

Meall Aonghais (Myowl Oonish, Angus's Hill) 42

Meall Bhaideanach (Myowl Vajenach, Hill of the Field of Sheep) 21

Meall Breac (Myowl Brechk, Trout Hill) 35

Meall Buidhe (Myowl *Boo*-ya, Yellow Hill) 7 (Beinn Achaladair), 45 (Glen Feshie)

Meall Coire Lochain (Myowl Corra Lochin, Hill of the Corrie of the Lochan) 29

Meall Dubh (Myowl Doo, Black Hill) 29

Meall Garbh (Myowl *Garra*v, Rough Hill) 10 (Glen Lyon), 13 (Beinn Sgilaird), 18 (Treig)

Meall Liath (Myowl *Lee*-a) Grey Hill 10

Meall na Cuartaige (Myowl Koo-*art*-iga, Hill of the Eddy) 24

Meall na Sroine (Myowl na *Strawn*a, Hill of the Nose) 26

Meall na Teanga (Myowl na *Tyeng*a, Hill of the Tongue) 29

Meall nan Aighean (Myowl nan Eggen, Hill of the Abyss) 10

Meall nan Ceapraichean (Myowl nan *Kep*richan, Hill of the Little Tops) 40

Meall nan Eun (Myowl nan *Yai*-awn, Bird Hill) 12

Meall nan Tri Tighearnan (Myowl nan Tree *Tee*-arnan, Hill of the Three Landlords) 12

Meall Odhar (Myowl *Oa*-ar, Dun-coloured Hill) 29

Oreval (Oraval, Grouse Mountain (from Norse *orri*), Water Mountain (from Norse *or*) or Orri's Mountain) 49

Sail Chaorainn (Sahl *Chœr*in, Rowan Heel) 35

Sail Dhubh (Sahl Ghoo, Black Heel) 8

Sgor Gaibhre (Skorr *Gav*ra, Goat Peak) 19

Sgor Gaoith (Skorr *Goo*-y, Wind Peak) 45

Sgor na h-Ulaidh (Skorr na Hooly, Peak of the Hidden Treasure) 15

Sgoran Dubh Mor (Beag) (Skorran Doo Moar (Beck), Big (Little) Black Peaklet) 45

Sgorr Craobh a' Chaorainn (Skorr Crœv a *Chœr*in, Peak of the Rowan Tree) 24

Sgorr nan Cearc (Skorr nan Kyairk, Peak of the Hens (i.e. Grouse)) 24

Sgorr nan Lochan Uaine (Skorr nan Lochan Oo-*an*-ya, Peak of the Green Lochan) 36

Sgurr a' Choire-bheithe (Skoor a Chorra *Vay*-ha, Peak of the Birch Corrie) 30

Sgurr a' Mhaoraich (Skoor a *Vœr*ich, Peak of the Shellfish) 33

Sgurr Airigh na Beinne (Skoor *Ai*-ry na *Ben*-ya, Peak of the Mountain Shieling) 30

Sgurr an Doire Leathain (Skoor an Jurra *Lyai*-in, Peak of the Broad Grove) 34

Sgurr an Fhuarain (Skoor an Oo-arin, Peak of the Spring) 28

Sgurr an Lochain (Skoor an Lochin, Peak of the Lochan) 34

Sgurr an t-Saighdeir (Skoor an Syjer, Peak of the Soldier) 20

Sgurr Beag (Skoor Beck, Little Peak) 34

Sgurr Breac (Skoor Brechk, Trout Peak) 39

Sgurr Coire na Feinne (Skoor Corra na *Fain*-ya, Peak of the Corrie of the Fingalians) 34

Sgurr Coire nan Eiricheallach (Skoor Corra nan Airich-*yall*ach, poss. Peak of the Corrie of the Rising (from Gaelic *eirich*) Charge (from Gaelic *eallach*)) 33

Sgurr Cos na Breachd-laoidh (Skoor Koas na Brechk *Lœ*-y, obscure; *cos* means foot, sponge or hole, *laoidh* means hymn, *breac* means trout, smallpox or speckled) 27

Sgurr Dhomhnuill (Skoor *Ghonn*il, Donald's Peak) 23

Sgurr Dubh (Skoor Doo, Black Peak) 36

Sgurr Mor (Beag) (Skoor Moar (Beck), Big (Little) Peak) 28

Sgurr na Ghiubhsachain (Skoor na *Ghyoo*sachin, Peak of the Fir Trees) 24

Sgurr na h-Aide (Skoor na Hejja, Hat Peak (named after its shape)) 26

Sgurr na h-Ighinn (Skoor na *Ee*yin, obscure; *igh* is tallow or stream, *ighean* is girl) 23

Sgurr nan Coireachan (Skoor nan *Corr*achan, Peak of the Corries) 27

Sgurr nan Conbhairean (Skoor nan *Conn*aviren, Peak of the Dog-men (i.e. hunters' attendants)) 35

Sron a' Choire Ghairbh (Strawn a Chorra *Ghirr*av, Nose of the Rough Corrie) 29

Sron Ard (Strawn Ard, Nose of the Height) 50

Sron Chona Choirein (Strawn Chonna Chorrin, Nose of the Adjoining Corrie or Corrie of Meeting) 9

Sron Gharbh (Strawn *Gharr*av, Rough Nose) 41

Sron Leachd a' Chaorainn (Strawn Lechkd a *Chœri*n, Slabby Nose of the Rowan) 19

Sron Lice na Fearna (Strawn *Leek*a na *Fyarn*a, Slabby Nose of the Alder) 30, 31

Sron na Garbh-bheinne, see Garbh-bheinn 18

Sron na Goibhre (Strawn na *Goy*ra, Nose of the Goat) 39

Sron nam Forsair (Strawn na Forser, Nose of the Forester) 16

Sron nan Eun (Strawn nan *Yai*-awn, Nose of the Bird) 8

Sron Scourst (obscure) 50

Sron Ulladale (Strawn Ooladale, Nose of Ulla's Dale) 49

Stacan Dubha (Stachkan *Doo*-a, Black Stack) 47

Sticil, The (Styeechkeel, The Beam) 47

Stob a' Ghlais Choire (Stop a Ghlass Corra, Peak of the Grey Corrie) 16

Stob an Fhuarain (Stop an *Oo*-arin, Peak of the Spring) 15

Stob Ban (Stop Bahn, White
Peak) 17

Stob Coir' an Albannaich (Stop
Corran *Ala*banach, Peak of
the Corrie of the Scotsman)
12

Stob Coire Sgriodain (Stop
Corra *Scree*jan, Peak of the
Corrie of Stones or Scree) 18

Stob Gaibhre (Stop *Gav*ra, Goat
Peak) 13

Stob Maol (Stop Mœl, Peak of
the Bare Hill) 11

Stob nan Clach (Stop nan Clach,
Stoney Peak) 8

Stob nan Coinnich Bhacain (Stop
nan *Coan*-yich *Vach*kin,
Peak of the Boggy Tether or
Notch) 1

Stuc Loch na Cabhaig (Stoochk
Loch na Cavik, Peak of the
Loch of Haste or Difficulty)
37

Stuchd an Lochain (Stoochk an
Lochin, Peak of the Lochan)
9

Teilesval (obscure; *val* is Norse
for peak) 50

Tigh Mor na Seilge (Ty Moar na
*Shal*aka, The Big House of
the Hunt) 35

Toll an Lochain (Toal an Lochin,
Hollow of the Lochan) 39

Toman Coinich (Toaman *Coan*-
yich, Boggy Knoll) 39

Uisgnaval Mor (*Oosh*gnaval
Moar, Big Oxen Peak) 50

Ullaval (Oolaval, Ulli's Peak) 49

Some other books published by **LUATH** PRESS

Joy of Hillwalking
Ralph Storer
ISBN 1 84282 069 9 PBK £7.50

Ralph Storer's highly entertaining exploration of the lure of the hills is underpinned by hard-won experience – he has climbed extensively in the British Isles, Europe and the American West, though his abiding love is the Scottish Highlands. His breezy anecdotes of walking and climbing around the world in all sorts of conditions are gripping and full of fun. This man has done more things in a sleeping bag than sleep, and in *The Joy of Hillwalking* he cheerfully tells all. His sense of humour is as irrepressible as his relish for adventurous ascents, but he doesn't have his head in the clouds when it comes to serious issues such as public access and conservation.

'Alps, America, Scandinavia, you name it – Storer's been there, so why the hell shouldn't he bring all these various and varied places into his observations... [He] even admits to losing his virginity after a day on the Aggy Ridge... a fine book... well worth its place beside Storer's earlier works.'
THE ANGRY CORRIE

'A light hearted and often highly amusing guide to the pleasures of the great outdoors.'
THE SCOTS MAGAZINE

'... the theory goes that, through an inexorable exchange of atoms, people who spend a lot of time riding bicycles become part bicycle. From all that hill hugging, could it be that Ralph Storer has transmogrified into part man, part hill – a hilluva man?'
SCOTTISH BOOK COLLECTOR

Of Big Hills and Wee Men
Peter Kemp
ISBN 1 84282 052 4 PBK £7.99

The big hills of Scotland are conquered by the wee men of Glasgow.

'Before us in the bright spring sunshine lay the entire Clyde valley, dominated by the vast sprawling mass of Glasgow, the dear green place. There was a time not too long ago when the old heavy industries would have made this view much less clear. But today we could see from the Cowal Hills and Greenock in the West to the Pentlands in the East.'

In this book, Peter Kemp traces his life from his early years in urban Glasgow to his adventures in the Scottish mountains. *Of Big Hills and Wee Men* sees Peter Kemp recount his tales of the mountains and of life growing up in Govan, tackling those two traditional images of Scotland – the shipyards and the glens.

From the time he bagged his first Munro, Peter Kemp has remained an enthusiastic hillwalker and this book is a testament to his passion for Scotland's outdoors and hillwalking culture. Accompanied by his life-long friends from Glasgow, he takes on the big hills of Scotland. This is a book for everyone who has found both escape and companionship amongst the mountains of Scotland.

Of Big Hills and Wee Men brings Scotland's natural world to life whether seeking to discover Scotland from an armchair or as an active hillwalker.

'Kemp is an engaging storyteller and has some good stories to tell... This is a great wee book.'
THE ANGRY CORRIE

Mountain Days & Bothy Nights

Dave Brown and Ian Mitchell

ISBN 0 946487 15 4 PBK £7.50

Acknowledged as a classic of mountain writing still in demand ten years after its first publication, this book takes you into the bothies, howffs and dosses on the Scottish hills. Fishgut Mac, Desperate Dan and Stumpy the Big Yin stalk hill and public house, evading gamekeepers and Royalty with a camaraderie which was the trademark of Scots hillwalking in the early days.

'The fun element comes through... how innocent the social polemic seems in our nastier world of today... the book for the rucksack this year.'

Hamish Brown, SCOTTISH MOUNTAINEERING CLUB JOURNAL

Scotland's Mountains before the Mountaineers

Ian Mitchell

ISBN 0 946487 39 1 PBK £9.99

In this ground-breaking book, Ian Mitchell tells the story of explorations and ascents in the Scottish Highlands in the days before mountaineering became a popular sport – when bandits, Jacobites, poachers and illicit distillers traditionally used the mountains as sanctuary. The book also gives a detailed account of the map makers, road builders, geologists, astrono-mers and naturalists, many of whom ascended hitherto untrodden summits while working in the Scottish Highlands.

Scotland's Mountains before the Mountaineers is divided into four Highland regions, with a map of each region showing key summits. While not designed primarily as a guide, it will be a useful handbook for walkers and climbers. Based on a wealth of new research, this book offers a fresh perspective that will fascinate climbers and mountaineers and everyone interested in the history of mountaineering, cartography, the evolution of landscape and the social history of the Scottish Highlands.

This is the most important book about Scottish mountaineering [since . . . 1988].

HIGH REVIEWS

The Highland Geology Trail

John L Roberts

ISBN 0946487 36 7 PBK £5.99

Where can you find the oldest rocks in Europe?

Where can you see ancient hills around 800 million years old?

How do you tell whether a valley was carved out by a glacier, not a river?

What are the Fucoid Beds?

Where do you find rocks folded like putty?

How did great masses of rock pile up like snow in front of a snow-plough?

When did volcanoes spew lava and ash to form Skye, Mull and Rum?

Where can you find fossils on Skye?

'...a lucid introduction to the geological record in general, a jargon-free exposition

of the regional background, and a series of descriptions of specific localities of geological interest on a 'trail' around the highlands.

Having checked out the local references on the ground, I can vouch for their accuracy and look forward to investigating farther afield, informed by this guide.

Great care has been taken to explain specific terms as they occur and, in so doing, John Roberts has created a resource of great value which is eminently usable by anyone with an interest in the outdoors... the best bargain you are likely to get as a geology book in the foreseeable future.'
Jim Johnston, PRESS AND JOURNAL

Skye 360: Walking the coastline of Skye

Andrew Dempster
ISBN 0 946487 85 5   PBK   £8.99

If you want to experience Skye in all its fascinating wealth of popular tourist haunts and hidden treasures, then let this book take you on a continuous 360-mile coastal walk around this enchanted island. You will soon find that there is a lot more to discover than the celebrated Cuillin ridge, mecca for walkers and climbers from all over the world.

Andrew Dempster took one month to walk the whole coastline. He describes not just a geographical journey along the intricacies of Skye's coast but also a historical journey from prehistoric fortified duns to legendary castles, from the distressing remains of blackhouses to the stark geometry of the Skye bridge.

Whether you want to follow the author on his month-long trek around the coast, or whether you have a week, a weekend or just want to spend a day exploring a smaller part of the island, *Skye 360* is the perfect guidebook.

Mountain Outlaw

Ian R Mitchell
ISBN 1 84282 027 3   £6.50

The amazing story of Ewan MacPhee, Scotland's last bandit.

In 1850 Ewan MacPhee of Glenquoich, these islands' last outlaw, died awaiting trial in jail in Fort William.

This was a man who:

- had been forced to enlist at the time of the Napoleonic wars, and deserted
- lived as an outlaw and rustler in Lochaber for over twenty years
- had several capital offences hanging over his head
- was a hero to the local peasantry at the time of the Clearances
- abducted a wife – who became his firmest ally in conflicts with the law

MacPhee has fascinated Ian R Mitchell for many years. He has sifted the surviving information on the outlaw, examined many of the legends associated with him, and bridged the gaps with an imagination of great authenticity, to produce Mountain Outlaw, a historical-creative account of MacPhee's life.

'The author has done a superb job in collating what little has been written about MacPhee... and has produced a mixture of fact and well-informed fiction to give us more than just a glimpse of the man's extraordinary life'.
SCOTS MAGAZINE

On the Trail of Queen Victoria in the Highlands

Ian R. Mitchell

ISBN 0 946487 79 0 UK £7.99

How many Munros did Queen Victoria bag?
What 'essential services' did John Brown perform for Victoria?
(and why was Albert always tired?)
How many horses (to the nearest hundred) were needed to undertake a Royal Tour?
What happens when you send a republican on the tracks of Queen Victoria in the Highlands?
• you get a book somewhat more interesting than the usual run of the mill royalist biographies!

Ian R. Mitchell took up the challenge of attempting to write with critical empathy on the peregrinations of Vikki Regina in the Highlands, and about her residence at Balmoral, through which a neo-feudal fairyland was created on Upper Deeside. The expeditions, social rituals and iconography of that world are explored and exploded from within, in what Mitchell terms a Bolshevisation of Balmorality. He follows in Victoria's footsteps throughout the Cairngorms and beyond, to the further reaches of the Highlands. On this journey, a grudging respect and even affection for Vikki ('the best of the bunch') emerges.

The book is designed to enable the armchair/motorised reader, or walker, to follow in the steps of the most widely-travelled royal personage in the Highlands since Bonnie Prince Charlie had wandered there a century earlier.

Index map and 12 detailed maps
21 walks in Victoria's footsteps
Rarely seen Washington Wilson photographs
Colour and black and white reproductions of contemporary paintings

On the Trail of Queen Victoria in the Highlands will also appeal to those with an interest in the social and cultural history of Scotland and the Highlands – and the author, ever-mindful of his own 'royalties', hopes the declining band of monarchists might also be persuaded to give the book a try. There has never been a book on Victoria like this. It is especially topical with the centenary of her death falling in 2001.

'entertaining and well researched... Mitchell, a distinguished historian with several books under his belt, writes with substantial first-hand experience of the rigours of walking in Scotland's more or less trackless spaces' THE TIMES

The Supernatural Highlands

Francis Thompson

ISBN 0 946487 31 6 PBK £8.99

An authoritative exploration of the otherworld of the Highlander, happenings and beings hitherto thought to be outwith the ordinary forces of nature. A simple introduction to the way of life of rural Highland and Island communities, this new edition weaves a path through second sight, the evil eye, witchcraft, ghosts, fairies and other supernatural beings, offering new sight-lines on areas of belief once dismissed as folklore and superstition.

But n Ben A-Go-Go
Matthew Fitt
ISBN 1 905222 04 1 PB £7.99

The year is 2090. Global flooding has left most of Scotland under water. The descendants of those who survived God's Flood live in a community of floating island parishes, known collectively as Port.

Port's citizens live in mortal fear of Senga, a supervirus whose victims are kept in a giant hospital warehouse in sealed capsules called Kists.

Paolo Broon is a low-ranking cyberjanny. His life-partner, Nadia, lies forgotten and alone in Omega Kist 624 in the Rigo Imbeki Medical Center. When he receives an unexpected message from his radge criminal father to meet him at But n Ben A-Go-Go, Paolo's life is changed forever.

He must traverse VINE, Port and the Drylands and deal with rebel American tourists and crabbit Dundonian microchips to discover the truth about his family's past in order to free Nadia from the sair grip of the merciless Senga.

Set in a distinctly unbonnie future-Scotland, the novel's dangerous atmosphere and psychologically-malkied characters weave a tale that both chills and intrigues.

'after a bit – not a very long bit – I was plunged into the particular language of this book just as I'm plunged into that of Chandler or Asimov… you can read this novel because it's very well-written, and it also tells a good story.'
W N HERBERT, SCOTLAND ON SUNDAY

'not a traditional rustic tale… I could understand quite a lot of that!' SUE MACGREGOR; *'the last man who tried anything like this was Hugh MacDiarmid'* MICHAEL FRY, TODAY PROGRAMME, BBC RADIO 4

'will wean young Scots off reading Harry Potter' RODDY MARTINE, DAILY MAIL

'a bit of a cracker. I have no Scots… and tend to avoid books with long passages in dialect. But I can, with occasional hiccups, read Fitt's offering and am doing so with much enjoyment. He has found the key, which is to eschew linguistic pedantry in favour of linguistic vigour. To hear him reading aloud at the book launch, giving the Scots language a modern literary voice without selfconsciousness or pretentiousness, was a mesmerising experience.'
KATIE GRANT, THE TIMES

'Easier to read than Shakespeare – twice the fun.' DES DILLON

The Whisky Muse
Robin Laing
ISBN 1 84282 041 9 PBK £7.99

This is a collection of the best poems and songs, both old and new, on the subject of that great Scottish love, whisky. Brought together by Robin Laing, a highly respected Scottish folk-singer and songwriter, and based on his one-man show *The Angel's Share*, it combines two of his passions – folk song and whisky. Each poem and song is accompanied by fascinating additional information, and the book is full of interesting tit-bits on the process of whisky making. Lubricated by warmth and companionship as well as a dram the Whisky Muse is the spark of inspiration that came to Scotland's great poets and songwriters. Slainte!

'This splendid book is necessary reading for anyone interested in whisky and song. It encapsulates Scottish folk culture and the very spirit of Scotland.' WHISKY MAGAZINE

'One of Scotland's premier folk singer-songwriters.' SUNDAY POST

WALK WITH LUATH

Walks in the Cairngorms
Ernest Cross
ISBN 0 946487 09 X PB £4.95

Short Walks in the Cairngorms
Ernest Cross
ISBN 0 946487 23 5 PB £4.95

LUATH GUIDES TO SCOTLAND

The North West Highlands: Roads to the Isles
Tom Atkinson
ISBN 1 84282 086 9 PB £5.99

Mull and Iona: Highways and Byways
Peter Macnab
ISBN 1 84282 089 3 PB £5.99

The Northern Highlands: The Empty Lands
Tom Atkinson
ISBN 1 84282 087 7 PB £5.99

The West Highlands: The Lonely Lands
Tom Atkinson
ISBN 1 84282 088 5 PB £5.99

ISLANDS

The Islands that Roofed the World: Easdale, Belnahua, Luing & Seil:
Mary Withall
ISBN 0 946487 76 6 PB £4.99

Rum: Nature's Island
Magnus Magnusson
ISBN 0 946487 32 4 PB £7.95

THE QUEST FOR

The Quest for the Celtic Key
Karen Ralls-MacLeod and Ian Robertson
ISBN 1 84282 084 2 PB £7.99

The Quest for the Nine Maidens
Stuart McHardy
ISBN 0 946487 66 9 HB £16.99

The Quest for Charles Rennie Mackintosh
John Cairney
ISBN 1 84282 058 3 HB £16.99

The Quest for Robert Louis Stevenson
John Cairney
ISBN 0 946487 87 1 HB £16.99

The Quest for the Original Horse Whisperers
Russell Lyon
ISBN 1 84282 020 6 HB £16.99

ON THE TRAIL OF

On the Trail of the Pilgrim Fathers
J. Keith Cheetham
ISBN 0 946487 83 9 PB £7.99

On the Trail of Mary Queen of Scots
J. Keith Cheetham
ISBN 0 946487 50 2 PB £7.99

On the Trail of John Wesley
J. Keith Cheetham
ISBN 1 84282 023 0 PB £7.99

On the Trail of William Wallace
David R. Ross
ISBN 0 946487 47 2 PB £7.99

On the Trail of Robert the Bruce
David R. Ross
ISBN 0 946487 52 9 PB £7.99

On the Trail of Robert Service
GW Lockhart
ISBN 0 946487 24 3 PB £7.99

On the Trail of John Muir
Cherry Good
ISBN 0 946487 62 6 PB £7.99

On the Trail of Robert Burns
John Cairney
ISBN 0 946487 51 0 PB £7.99

On the Trail of Bonnie Prince Charlie
David R Ross
ISBN 0 946487 68 5 PB £7.99

On the Trail of Scotland's Myths and Legends
Stuart McHardy
ISBN 1 84282 049 4 PB £7.99

TRAVEL & LEISURE

**Die Kleine Schottlandfibel
[Scotland Guide in German]**
Hans-Walter Arends
ISBN 0 946487 89 8 PB £8.99

Let's Explore Berwick-upon-Tweed
Anne Bruce English
ISBN 1 84282 029 X PB £4.99

Let's Explore Edinburgh Old Town
Anne Bruce English
ISBN 0 946487 98 7 PB £4.99

Edinburgh's Historic Mile
Duncan Priddle
ISBN 0 946487 97 9 PB £2.99

Pilgrims in the Rough: St Andrews beyond the 19th hole
Michael Tobert
ISBN 0 946487 74 X PB £7.99

NATURAL WORLD

The Hydro Boys: pioneers of renewable energy
Emma Wood
ISBN 1 84282 047 8 PB £8.99

Wild Scotland
James McCarthy
photographs by Laurie Campbell
ISBN 0 946487 37 5 PB £8.99

Wild Lives: Otters – On the Swirl of the Tide
Bridget MacCaskill
ISBN 0 946487 67 7 PB £9.99

Wild Lives: Foxes – The Blood is Wild
Bridget MacCaskill
ISBN 0 946487 71 5 PB £9.99

**Scotland – Land & People:
An Inhabited Solitude**
James McCarthy
ISBN 0 946487 57 X PB £7.99

The Highland Geology Trail
John L Roberts
ISBN 0 946487 36 7 PB £5.99

Red Sky at Night
John Barrington
ISBN 0 946487 60 X PB £8.99

Listen to the Trees
Don MacCaskill
ISBN 0 946487 65 0 PB £9.99

FOLKLORE

Tall Tales from an Island
Peter Macnab
ISBN 0 946487 07 3 PB £8.99

GENEALOGY

Scottish Roots: step-by-step guide for ancestor hunters
Alwyn James
ISBN 1 84282 090 7 PB £6.99

SPORT

Over the Top with the Tartan Army
Andy McArthur
ISBN 0 946487 45 6 PB £7.99

Ski & Snowboard Scotland
Hilary Parke
ISBN 0 946487 35 9 PB £6.99

FICTION

Selected Stories
Dilys Rose
ISBN 1 84282 077 X PB £7.99

Lord of Illusions
Dilys Rose
ISBN 1 84282 076 1 PB £7.99

Torch
Lin Anderson
ISBN 1 84282 042 7 PB £9.99

Heartland
John MacKay
ISBN 1 84282 059 1 PB £9.99

The Blue Moon Book
Anne MacLeod
ISBN 1 84282 061 3 PB £9.99

The Glasgow Dragon
Des Dillon
ISBN 1 84282 056 7 PB £9.99

Driftnet
Lin Anderson
ISBN 1 84282 034 6 PB £9.99

The Fundamentals of New Caledonia
David Nicol
ISBN 1 84282 93 6 HB £16.99

Milk Treading
Nick Smith
ISBN 1 84282 037 0 PB £6.99

The Kitty Killer Cult
Nick Smith
ISBN 1 84282 039 7 PB £9.99

The Road Dance
John MacKay
ISBN 1 84282 024 9 PB £6.99

The Strange Case of RL Stevenson
Richard Woodhead
ISBN 0 946487 86 3 HB £16.99

The Bannockburn Years
William Scott
ISBN 0 946487 34 0 PB £7.95

Outlandish Affairs: An Anthology of Amorous Encounters
Edited and introduced by Evan Rosenthal and Amanda Robinson
ISBN 1 84282 055 9 PB £9.99

Six Black Candles
Des Dillon
ISBN 1 84282 053 2 PB £6.99

Me and Ma Gal
Des Dillon
ISBN 1 84282 054 0 PB £5.99

POETRY

Burning Whins
Liz Niven
ISBN 1 84282 074 5 PB £8.99

Drink the Green Fairy
Brian Whittingham
ISBN 1 84282 020 6 PB £8.99

Tartan & Turban
Bashabi Fraser
ISBN 1 84282 044 3 PB £8.99

The Ruba'iyat of Omar Khayyam, in Scots
Rab Wilson
ISBN 1 84282 046 X PB £8.99

Talking with Tongues
Brian D. Finch
ISBN 1 84282 006 0 PB £8.99

Kate o Shanter's Tale and other poems [book]
Matthew Fitt
ISBN 1 84282 028 1 PB £6.99

Kate o Shanter's Tale and other poems [audio CD]
Matthew Fitt
ISBN 1 84282 043 5 PB £9.99

Bad Ass Raindrop
Kokumo Rocks
ISBN 1 84282 018 4 PB £6.99

Madame Fifi's Farewell and other poems
Gerry Cambridge
ISBN 1 84282 005 2 PB £8.99

Poems to be Read Aloud
introduced by Tom Atkinson
ISBN 0 946487 00 6 PB £5.00

Scots Poems to be Read Aloud
introduced by Stuart McHardy
ISBN 0 946487 81 2 PB £5.00

Picking Brambles
Des Dillon
ISBN 1 84282 021 4 PB £6.99

Sex, Death & Football
Alistair Findlay
ISBN 1 84282 022 2 PB £6.99

The Luath Burns Companion
John Cairney
ISBN 1 84282 000 1 PB £10.00

Immortal Memories: A Compilation of Toasts to the Memory of Burns as delivered at Burns Suppers, 1801-2001
John Cairney
ISBN 1 84282 009 5 HB £20.00

A Long Stride Shortens the Road
Donald Smith
ISBN 1 84282 073 7 PB £8.99

Into the Blue Wavelengths
Roderick Watson
ISBN 1 84282 075 3 PB £8.99

The Souls of the Dead are Taking the Best Seats: 50 World Poets on War
Compiled by Angus Calder and Beth Junor
ISBN 1 84282 032 X PB £7.99

Sun Behind the Castle
Angus Calder
ISBN 1 84282 078 8 PB £8.99

FOOD & DRINK

First Foods Fast: how to prepare good simple meals for your baby
Lara Boyd
ISBN 1 84282 002 8 PB £4.99

BIOGRAPHY

Not Nebuchadnezzar: In search of identities
Jenni Calder
ISBN 1 84282 060 5 PB £9.99

The Last Lighthouse
Sharma Krauskopf
ISBN 0 946487 96 0 PB £7.99

Tobermory Teuchter
Peter Macnab
ISBN 0 946487 41 3 PB £7.99

Bare Feet & Tackety Boots
Archie Cameron
ISBN 0 946487 17 0 PB £7.95

Come Dungeons Dark
John Taylor Caldwell
ISBN 0 946487 19 7 PB £6.95

SOCIAL HISTORY

Pumpherston: the story of a shale oil village
Sybil Cavanagh
ISBN 1 84282 011 7 HB £17.99
ISBN 1 84282 015 X PB £10.99

Shale Voices
Alistair Findlay
ISBN 0 946487 78 2 HB £17.99
ISBN 0 946487 63 4 PB £10.99

A Word for Scotland
Jack Campbell
ISBN 0 946487 48 0 PB £12.99

Crofting Years
Francis Thompson
ISBN 0 946487 06 5 PB £6.95

Hail Philpstoun's Queen
Barbara and Marie Pattullo
ISBN 1 84282 095 8 PB £6.99

HISTORY

Spectacles, testicles, fags and matches: WWII RAF Commandos
Tom Atkinson
ISBN 1 84282 071 0 PB £12.99

Desire Lines: A Scottish Odyssey
David R Ross
ISBN 1 84282 033 8 PB £9.99

Scots in Canada
Jenni Calder
ISBN 1 84282 038 9 PB £7.99

Civil Warrior: extraordinary life & poems of Montrose
Robin Bell
ISBN 1 84282 013 3 HB £10.99

LANGUAGE

Luath Scots Language Learner [Book]
L Colin Wilson
ISBN 0 946487 91 X PB £9.99

Luath Scots Language Learner [Double Audio CD Set]
L Colin Wilson
ISBN 1 84282 026 5 CD £16.99

POLITICS AND CURRENT ISSUES

Getting it Together: the Campaign for a Scottish Assembly/Parliament
Bob McLean
ISBN 1 905222 02 5 PB £12.99

Agenda for a New Scotland: Visions of Scotland 2020
Edited by Kenny MacAskill
ISBN 1 905222 00 9 PB £9.99

Scotlands of the Mind
Angus Calder
ISBN 1 84282 008 7 PB £9.99

Building a Nation: Post Devolution Nationalism In Scotland
Kenny MacAskill
ISBN 1 84282 081 8 PB £4.99

Scotlands of the Future: Sustainability in a Small Nation
Edited by Eurig Scandrett
ISBN 1 84282 035 4 PB £7.99

Luath Press Limited
committed to publishing well written books worth reading

LUATH PRESS takes its name from Robert Burns, whose little collie Luath (Gael., swift or nimble) tripped up Jean Armour at a wedding and gave him the chance to speak to the woman who was to be his wife and the abiding love of his life. Burns called one of The Twa Dogs Luath after Cuchullin's hunting dog in Ossian's Fingal. Luath Press was established in 1981 in the heart of Burns country, and is now based a few steps up the road from Burns' first lodgings on Edinburgh's Royal Mile.

Luath offers you distinctive writing with a hint of unexpected pleasures.

Most bookshops in the UK, the US, Canada, Australia, New Zealand and parts of Europe either carry our books in stock or can order them for you. To order direct from us, please send a £sterling cheque, postal order, international money order or your credit card details (number, address of cardholder and expiry date) to us at the address below. Please add post and packing as follows: UK – £1.00 per delivery address; overseas surface mail – £2.50 per delivery address; overseas airmail – £3.50 for the first book to each delivery address, plus £1.00 for each additional book by airmail to the same address. If your order is a gift, we will happily enclose your card or message at no extra charge.

Luath Press Limited
543/2 Castlehill
The Royal Mile
Edinburgh EH1 2ND
Scotland
Telephone: 0131 225 4326 (24 hours)
Fax: 0131 225 4324
email: gavin.macdougall@luath.co.uk
Website: www.luath.co.uk